JUXTASEVEN

Research and Scholarship in Haiku

2021

THE Haiku FOUNDATION

JUXTASEVEN

ISBN 978-0-9826951-8-0
Copyright © 2021 by The Haiku Foundation

JUXTASEVEN is the print version of *Juxtapositions* 7.1.
A journal of haiku research and scholarship,
Juxtapositions is published by The Haiku Foundation.

The Haiku Foundation
PO Box 2461
Winchester VA
22604-1661 USA
www.thehaikufoundation.org/juxta

SENIOR EDITOR
Ce Rosenow

GENERAL EDITORS
Stephen Addiss
Josh Hockensmith
Adam L. Kern
Crystal Simone Smith

REVIEW EDITOR
David Grayson

HAIGA EDITOR
Stephen Addiss

MANAGING EDITOR
Jim Kacian

TECHNICAL MANAGER
Dave Russo

Contents

Editor's Welcome .... Ce Rosenow 7

   Haiga: "The Paradigm" .... Amiri Baraka 9

A Certain Tightness in the Chest .... Adam L. Kern 11

   Haiga: "Culture" .... Amiri Baraka 89

Living in Community .... Amanda Monteleone 91

   Haiga: "Was It Ever" .... Amiri Baraka 121

The Haiku in Amiri Baraka's Low Coup Crystal Simone Smith 123

   Haiga: "Heaven Appeared" .... Amiri Baraka 135

Reading Classical Chinese Poetry .... Jianqing Zheng 137

   Haiga: "1 + 1 = 1" .... Amiri Baraka 151

Recent Dissertations on Haiku .... Josh Hockensmith 153

   Haiga: "Animal Scientist" .... Amiri Baraka 165

The Pleasures and Heartbreaks of the Road .... Adam L. Kern 167

Appreciation and Appropriation .... J. Zimmerman 175

Rain, Sake, and the Moon .... J. Zimmerman 183

Modern Matters .... Keith Ekiss 191

   Haiga: "Low Coup" .... Amiri Baraka 199

Juxta Contributors 201

Juxta Staff 203

Editor's Welcome

I am pleased to welcome you to *Juxtapositions* 7, an issue rich in its presentation of scholarship, art, resources, and reviews.

Each essay submitted to *Juxtapositions* undergoes a rigorous process of blind peer review. Many essays are rejected or returned for significant revision and the invitation to resubmit them. Others are accepted with minor revisions, and a limited number are accepted with no additional revision requirements. We have four fine essays in *Juxtapositions* 7, and I'm delighted to say that two of them are by members of the editorial board: Adam Kern's "A Certain Tightness in the Chest: *Sarasen* (Salaryman *Senryū*) on 3-11, Covid-19, the 2020 Tokyo Olympics, and Other Such Catastrophes" and Crystal Simone Smith's "The Haiku in Amiri Baraka's Low Coup." Their work is joined by Amanda Monteleone's essay, "Living in Community: The More-than-Human World in Gerald Vizenor's Haiku," and Jianqing Zheng's essay, "Reading Classical Chinese Poetry with a Haiku Mind: A Writing Practice."

This issue also includes a very special addition: Black folk art by Amiri Baraka, with examples referenced in Crystal Simone Smith's essay. The images are printed with permission of Ishmael Reed Publishing Company. We are grateful to Ishmael Reed and Tennessee Reed. With the images' similarity to haiga and relevance to Smith's article, they are an exciting and important addition to the issue in place of the haiga usually published here.

As always, we strive to include information about resources that will aid scholars researching haiku-related topics. Josh Hockensmith, also on the editorial board, built on a previous annotated bibliography created by former editor, Randy M. Brooks, adding entries for the most current scholarship in the field.

Finally, we round out the issue with four book reviews arranged by Book Review Editor, David Grayson: *Matsuo Bashō: Travel Writings* by Steven D. Carter (reviewer Adam Kern); *The Life and Zen Haiku Poetry of Santoka Taneda* by Oyama Sumita and translated by William Scott Wilson (reviewer J. Zimmerman); *American Haiku: New Readings* by Toru Kiuchi (reviewer J. Zimmerman); and *American Haiku, Eastern Philosophies, and Modernist Poetics* by Yoshinobu Hakutani (reviewer Keith Ekiss).

Juxtapositions would not be in its seventh year and preparing for its eighth without the work of the editorial board members past and present, Managing Editor Jim Kacian, and The Haiku Foundation for supporting what continues to be the only English-language, peer-reviewed journal of haiku scholarship.

Please enjoy *Juxtapositions* 7.

Ce Rosenow
Senior Editor

Poet/Artist: Amiri Baraka

A Certain Tightness in the Chest:
Sarasen (salaryman *Senryū* on 3-11, Covid-19, the 2020 Tokyo Olympics, and Other Such Catastophes

Adam L. Kern

ABSTRACT: This article presents annotated translations of Japanese salaryman *senryū* — referred to affectionately in Japanese as *sarasen* — written over the past decade or so on the topic of various national traumas. These traumas include the Fukushima triple disaster, the COVID-19 pandemic, and the troubled 2020 Tokyo Olympics. Comparing the authorship of eighteenth-century *senryū* with that of these *sarasen* yields some important conclusions about the supposed anonymity of the former and the changing nature of the latter. Specifically, contrary to the received wisdom, early modern Japanese *senryū* were not, as a rule, anonymous. And modern *sarasen* frequently deploy short-lived pen names that provide an additional resource for overcoming the brevity of the 17-syllable verseform. We also see a conspicuous shift from indirect to overt satire that reflects the change from early modern authoritarian state to modern constitutionally based democratic monarchy.

Sarasen Then and Now

It has been two long decades since Richard Gardner published his classic English-language essay on *sararīman senryū*, or "salaryman *senryū*," essentially a kind of comic haiku popular in contemporary Japan. Although "salaryman" as an English loanword into Japanese normally refers to the salaried employee at a company, in this context the word has come to stand more broadly for the average adult member of society, even those who are not, per se, salaried. As a modern outgrowth of the *senryū* of Japan's early modern period (also known as the Edo or Tokugawa period, 1600 – 1868), the salaryman *senryū* typically presents the wisdom of the crowd in three phrases of 5 then 7 then 5 Japanese "syllabets" (*on*) — "syllabet" not quite corresponding to the English syllable.[1] Most such 17-syllabet verses playfully expose inconsistencies in common sense or the façade of sociopolitical reality, if not excavate hidden truths about existence itself, sometimes transcending the particulars of time and place, thereby achieving a kind of universality, not unlike the best haiku, for that matter.

Precisely because so much time has elapsed since Gardner's article, myriad topical issues have come and gone. Some of them, regrettably, deep traumas that make one feel, to borrow a phrase from one verse translated herein, "a certain tightness in the chest." Moreover, our knowledge of early modern *senryū* itself has changed. The moment therefore seems propitious to revisit the salaryman *senryū* — or *sarasen*, as it is more succinctly, widely, and affectionately referred to in Japanese, combining the first two syllabets of both words (though Gardner himself did not use this truncated slang). The present article, then, situates *sarasen* in the larger context of early modern Japanese *senryū*, drawing on recent examples in lightly annotated translation.[2]

---

1. For a discussion of the term "syllabet," see Kern, pp. xxxvii and lxxvi-lxxvii. For a discussion of the terms *on* and *onji*, see Gilbert.
2. All translations are my own. The early modern verses were previously published in Kern.

Specifically, I argue three interrelated points. First, while there is tremendous continuity in *senryū* from early-modern to present-day Japan, including a strain of what can be described as sociopolitical commentary if not satire, one striking development has been the transformation of the penname into an additional resource for overcoming the brevity of the 17-syllabet format. This development, exciting in its own right, begs rethinking of the conventional wisdom that the early modern *senryū* itself was anonymous. Second, and somewhat not unrelatedly, the directness of sociopolitical satire over the preceding couple of centuries has increased conspicuously, particularly in the past few decades. Although this increase is due mainly to Japan's transformation from authoritarian state to constitutionally based democratic monarchy, the rise of the tailored penname has also played a pivotal role. It might even be said that the use of such pennames has authorized the spike in barbed satire. Third and finally, with the slump in newspaper editorial cartooning of late, particularly in addressing national traumas, the *sarasen* has emerged as perhaps the leading mode of mainstream sociopolitical satire in contemporary Japan. This development has been largely overlooked, it is worth speculating, because the *senryū* is still generally overshadowed by the modern haiku.

Properly speaking, sarasen is most closely associated with one specific annual competition, sponsored by the Dai-Ichi Life Insurance Company (Daiichi Seimei Hoken Kabushiki Gaisha). There are other similar competitions, to be sure, effectively turning *sarasen* into an eponym (just as the Band-Aid brand name has come to signify bandages more generically). Still, Dai-Ichi Life can claim not only having coined the term, but also sponsoring the largest, best-known, and longest-running competition open to the general public. The 34th such contest, held in 2020 from September to October, attracted 62,542 entries from all around Japan. Assuming one entry per person, that's roughly one submission for every 2,020

Japanese people. Comparing apples to *mikan*, one in every 61,094 Americans enters the *New Yorker* magazine cartoon captioning contest per issue.[3] All told, the average American is about thirty times less likely to participate in the weekly *New Yorker* cartoon captioning contest, by this reckoning, than the average Japanese person is likely to submit a *sarasen* to the annual Dai-Ichi Life contest. This rough comparison suggests the relative popularity of *sarasen* in general and this contest in particular.

In the 2020 contest, the top 100 semifinalist verses — many of which have been translated for the present article — were announced in January 2021.[4] Then, befitting modern Japanese democracy, more than 100,000 *sarasen* fans nationwide voted, the ranked results being announced in May 2021. Merely making this list is regarded as quite the accomplishment. This year's winner garnered 4,322 votes — some 876 more than the first runner up.

As might be expected, given the topical nature of *senryū*, many of the verses in the 2020 contest addressed the Covid-19 pandemic. Particularly the pleasures and pains of telecommuting and mask wearing. Yet there was also some criticism leveled at the Japanese government for its prolonged and anemic response to the crisis. The criticism was made all the more biting by direct mention of politicians by name and, perhaps surprisingly, in some cases by mocking nickname. Additionally, just as early modern *senryū* often drew and commented on contemporary popular culture, especially

---

3. These figures are based on the latest data available: approximately 126,300,000 Japanese versus 328,200,000 Americans, and 62,542 submissions to the 34th Dai-Ichi Life contest versus an average of 5,372 weekly entries to the cartoon captioning contest. This last figure is quoted in Bob Mankoff, "Seven Reasons It's Hard to Win the Caption Contest," in *The New Yorker*, November 8, 2014. Accessed online at https://www.newyorker.com/cartoons/bob-mankoff/seven-reasons-why-hard-to-win-caption-contest.
4. Press release, Dai-ichi Life Insurance Company, May 2021. https://event.dai-ichi-life.co.jp/company/senryu/. Accessed May 2021. All demographics and statistics related to the 2020 contest cited herein come from this source unless otherwise mentioned.

the so-called "floating world" of pleasure quarters, street spectacles, and kabuki theater—not to omit closely associated woodblock-printed pictures (*ukiyo-e*) and comicbooks (*kusazōshi*)—so too did these *sarasen* reference such things as animated films (*anime*), comics and graphic novels (*manga*), J-pop music, and so on. While the attention to popular culture occasioned some good-natured mocking of generational divides, demographic information provided in the Dai-Ichi Life press release seems to suggest that the best verses actually speak to multiple age groups, at least among those who voted. We also find that the authors varied in age as well. These data points help further corroborate the widespread popularity of *sarasen* in contemporary Japan.

Most of the *sarasen* translated herein, unless otherwise noted, come from this most recent Dai-Ichi Life contest. However, for the purposes of this article, I have also dipped into some other contests, websites, and blogs, specifically: the online forum "Minna de Seiji Senryū" (Let's All Do Political *Senryū*)[5]; "Marusen" (a weekly *sarasen* contest)[6]; "3.11 Hinansha Senryū" (3-11 Evacuee *Senryū*)[7]; "Tamura Akiko's *Senryū* Blog"[8]; and the portal site of Miyagi Prefecture, host to some events of the postponed 2020 Tokyo Olympics.[9]

As for the early modern *senryū* herein, almost all come from the main repository of such verses, *Haifū Yanagidaru* (*The Willowwood Vat, Haikai Style*, 1765 to 1840).[10] *Yanagidaru*, as it is frequently called, was a massive collection of standalone *senryū*, in 167 volumes published over 75 years, judged and selected by Karai Senryū (1718–1790) and edited by Goryōken Arubeshi (d. 1788),

---

5. http://www.fujii-hiroki.net/senryuuBBS/epad.cgi?fbclid=IwAR2TIkXohZFvFLk2pyRm69e3hon4OS3jlPqrNDlMSYL_fuHWNfosYk_vS-U.
6. https://marusenryu.com/.
7. http://sandori2014.blog.fc2.com/blog-category-26.html.
8. https://shinyokan.jp/senryu-blogs/akiko/20532/.
9. https://www.pref.miyagi.jp/site/olympic/olyparamiyagisenryu.html.
10. See Okada.

then after their deaths by many others (some of whom adopted the Karai Senryū moniker). The centrality and significance of this collection cannot be understated. For one thing, *Yanagidaru* helped popularize 17-syllabet verseform as a single standalone verse, making the *senryū* — rather than the haiku — the first such verse in Japan, if not the world, to be mass-published and widely circulated to large segments of the population with little or no lag time. For another thing, this standalone verse would come to assume the name of the main judge of the verses collected in *Yanagidaru* — or at least his penname.

A Penname by Any Other Name

Taking the three abovementioned main points in order, one of the surprising continuities in *senryū* composition from the eighteenth century to the present day is the use of pennames. In order to explore this continuity and assess a significant modulation within it, however — and at the risk of digressing at length from *sarasen* — it should first be observed that the very existence of pennames would seem to fly in the face of the conventional thinking that early modern *senryū* were anonymous.

This conventional thinking, put forth in works of popular Japanese scholarship, has regrettably taken hold in English-language writings on the topic. Consider the following statements by some of the leading experts on Japanese haiku and/or *senryū* (who anglicize the latter without a long mark and/or italics), most of whom seem to follow in the footsteps of amateur scholar-translator Reginald Horace Blyth. Blyth, in his book *Senryu* (1949), contended that the main distinction between early modern and modern *senryū* was anonymity: "When senryu have no author given, they are old senryu, anonymous" (1). Blyth even doubled down, stating unequivocally: "The anonymity of early senryu is a strange but significant characteristic. It suggests an indifference to fame, and a cooperative creative urge without parallel in the annals of modern literature" (56).

Most scholars have followed Blyth's lead. Donald Keene, in *World Within Walls* (1978), discussing what he generalized as "the anonymous, communal nature of senryū," asserted that it was only in the nineteenth century that "some senryū poets began to affix their names to their compositions . . ." as if to suggest that attribution was the modern exception that proved the rule of anonymity in earlier *senryū* (528). Similarly, Haruo Shirane, in *Early Modern Japanese Literature* (2002), has observed: "Today about 200,000 senryū from the middle to the end of the Tokugawa period survive, but almost all of them are anonymous . . ." (522). Stephen Addiss, writing about mid-eighteenth century *senryū* in *The Art of Haiku* (2012), has likewise noted "at this time senryu were almost always anonymous" (156). Finally, Makoto Ueda, in *Light Verse from the Floating World: An Anthology of Premodern Japanese Senryu* (1999), finessed the conventional wisdom ever so slightly: "Little is known about the identities of those who wrote senryu in premodern Japan." The reason being, apparently, that the names of authors were regularly withheld when submitting these verses to contests in order to ensure "impartiality" (14).

Now, to say that the early modern *senryū* was anonymous is not entirely accurate. It is true that the real names of the authors of early modern *senryū* were rarely if ever published outright alongside their verses. And it may well be that some judges evaluated verses blindly, without any authorial identification. Yet this hardly means that these verses were "anonymous." In point of fact, the vast majority of early modern *senryū* were rarely if ever composed, submitted, or published anonymously, without any name attached. As a rule, *senryū* bore some kind of penname as opposed to the anonym "author unknown" (*yomihito shirazu*) or no name whatsoever.

Actually, we see the inclusion of pennames in the very roots of *senryū*: from the very earliest mass-printed publications of the versecapping contests that would eventually yield freestanding *senryū*, such as Tachiba Fukaku's (1662 – 1753) foundational *Futaba no matsu* (*Two-Needle Pine*, 1690) and *Hanabatake* (*Blossom Field*, 1711).[11] And we certainly see pennames in *Yanagidaru*, which, at the risk of redundancy, is the chief repository of early modern *senryū*. There are many other *senryū* collections from the period, yet they pale in comparison to *Yanagidaru* in terms of magnitude, popularity, stature, and influence. Furthermore, it is worth keeping in mind that the very term *senryū* itself derives from the penname of the main judge of *Yanagidaru*, a low-ranking government official whose "real" name was Karai Hachiemon.

Looking at all 167 volumes of *Yanagidaru*, on first blush the individual verses in volumes 1-9 (1765 – 1774) appear to bear no discernible authorial penname. Yet this fact cannot be taken to mean that the identities of the authors of the verses in volumes 1-9 were completely unknown to the compilers or editors. Ueda's suggestion of impartiality at the stage of judging aside, the omission of pennames in the resultant publication was probably a space-saving device, especially given the cramped layout of *Yanagidaru* volumes. Still, even in these early volumes, the trend was progressively toward the inclusion of pennames. Setting aside the possibility that a small number of authors embedded their pennames within their verses — Bashō did as much in a verse from another collection, as we shall see — on closer inspection, we find the pennames if not the actual names of some contributors appearing at the beginning of volumes 6 (1771) and 8 (1773).

Furthermore, a small number of verses published without pennames in these early volumes, or in the earlier versecapping collections with which they were associated, sometimes were published elsewhere with pennames. Just because a verse was

---

11. In Hamada, NKBZ 46, 271.

published anonymously in one place does not mean it was published anonymously everywhere else. While it is theoretically possible that two people independently wrote exactly the same verse by coincidence, to have that verse selected in two or more contests seems exponentially unlikely. More probably, such cases are instances of piracy, in which someone effectively claims authorship of an already published verse under false pretenses. After all, There are plenty of cases in *Yanagidaru* alone in which the same verse appears under two or more pennames.

> the other breast!
> the first stirrings of desire
> does grabbing it beget!
>
> *katachibusa / nigiru ga yoku no / deki hajime*

This verse first appeared in *Yanagidaru* 26 (1796) by one Jinsei. Nearly identical versions would be published later by two other named poets, Rekisen in *Yanagidaru* 58 (1811) and Gan'en in *Yanagidaru* 59 (1812).

One verse was even republished an unprecedented two times within the very same volume, *Yanagidaru* 106 (1829):

> for his peccadillos
> to the bordello he goes,
> the fool gung-ho!
>
> *machigae de / imo no ha e noru / baka mōja*

The surface meaning of this complex verse is deceptively simple: "by mistake / boarding the leaf of a potato, / foolish lost soul!" Yet there is some deeper wordplay. The key to the puzzle is that the only kind of potato (*imo*) whose leaf visually resembles the pad of the lotus—associated in Buddhism with rebirth and purity—is the taro root plant (*satoimo*). The word omitted from the verse being *sato* (village), slang for "pleasure quarters," secondary meanings of *machigae*, "blunder," as "sexual indiscretion" (contrasting ironically with purity), and *mōja*, "the deceased," as "aficionado," come to the fore. Additionally, the two graphs for *baka* (fool), "horse" and "deer," connote dumb beasts—the state of existence into which great sinners were said to be reborn. More than an inability to differentiate between lotus and taro, then, it is his asinine attachment to sensual pleasures that prevents this player from ever reaching paradise.

The first appearance of this verse in *Yanagidaru* 106 is by one Ryūsen. There is no way of knowing whether Ryūsen was the first of the three to write the verse, but let's assume for the sake of discussion he was. Since the other two poets could not have pirated Ryūsen's *senryū* from the same volume in which their poems appear, either they saw the winning verse in an earlier collection, or else all three poets, including Ryūsen, pirated the verse from an earlier source, either by Ryūsen or someone else. It is possible, in other words, that Ryūsen *himself* submitted the same verse to multiple contests and was lucky enough to have won at least two of them. Some combination of these scenarios is also possible. The wordplay in this particular verse being so complex, however, it seems completely out of the question for two, let alone three, different poets to have arrived on the same identical verse independently by coincidence. Hence, the triple appearance of this poem within the same volume of *Yanagidaru* is a clear case of literary piracy, perhaps even self-piracy.

It is also possible that the republication of a verse may have disclosed the penname of the author who was unnamed in an original publication. Either way, by volume 12 (1777), pennames were attached to almost all specific verses—a practice that characterizes the remaining 155 volumes (up to 1840). Over the 75 years of the publication of the 167 volumes of *Yanagidaru*, only a dozen volumes over a dozen years lacked pennames.

In the case of major contributors, information over and above their pennames is sometimes included separately, often early on within the volume, as with addresses, or names of their hometowns, or information about their poetry clubs.[12] Volume 12, which largely set the pattern to come, contains a prefatory page, arranging major contributors into three tiers, denoted by different mountain crests, in descending order of quality, as we see in Figure 1:

> First tier: Hasse from Ichigae Tamachi; Ryūsui from Asabu Eizaka; Tsurgame from Koshigawa Hakusan; Sakuragi from Upper Yamashita. Second tier (the second and third rows): Miyuki from Ushikomi; Wakana from Shinbori; Kakitsubata from Kanda; Kiyotaki from Yotsuya; Masago from Aoyama; Takane from Sakurada; Hatsune from Kōshichō; Kanko from Ōtenma; Nobori from Senjū; Iroha from Shitaya; Imasu from Imado; Yōrō from Kohinata; Kabukto from Hachōbori; Maizuru from Koshigawa; Suisen from Nihon'enoki. And third tier: Fūzetsu from Maruyama; Hagoromo from Kanda; Tachibana from Tachibanachō; Asahi from Yagenbori; Ōtsue from Yanagihara; and Tamagawa from Mita.

In summary, although further study of other collections may eventually provide an even more fine-grained picture, in the meantime, to the extent that *Yanagidaru* is any indication, there can be little question that most early modern *senryū* used pennames. The conventional view that early modern 12 pt were anonymous, then, either disregards this preponderance of pennames, or else assumes that pennames engender anonymity. If the latter is true, then why does the use of pennames in haiku not likewise engender anonymity?

---

12. Scholar Suzuki Katsutada has observed that many *senryū* pennames incorporate a reference to the faction or school one belonged to — a practice not dissimilar to haiku pennames. In Suzuki, 'Kaisetsu,' in NKBZ 46, 213.

SEVEN

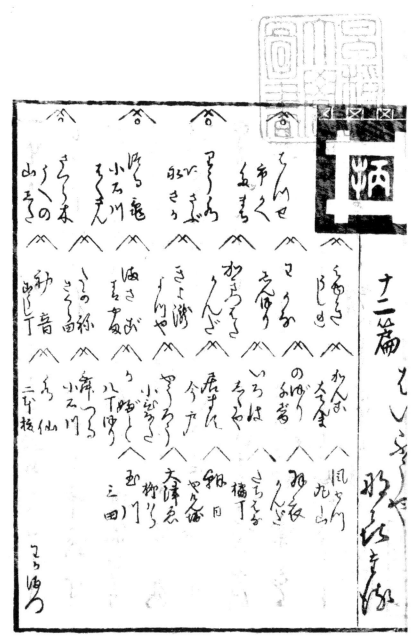

Fig 1 *Yanagidaru* 12 author page before works cited.

Conversely, the view that *senryū* were anonymous seems correct only so far as pennames actually hid the real identity of authors. However, there is good reason to believe they did not. I would suggest that the conventional wisdom unfortunately suffers both from some binary thinking that pits haiku against *senryū* in a kind of zero-sum game, as well as from the imposition of some present-day attitudes toward pennames, fame, and anonymity onto those of early modern Japan. In order to unravel this Gordian knot, let us take these two points in reverse order.

Pseudonym vs. Heteronym

The conventional thinking would seem to presume that pennames function primarily as pseudonyms, aliases meant to shield an individual's social identity from the public and hence from the authorities. This certainly appears to be the case when elite members of society, such as samurai, used pennames to compose 17-syllabet verse, rather than using their real names to compose the supposedly more dignified 31-syllabet *waka* or *tanka* that the government officially favored. The use of such pseudonyms allowed elites to compose haiku, *senryū*, and even dirty sexy haiku (*bareku*) without immediate discovery by their superiors. Scholar Hamada Giichirō has pointed out that samurai bannermen (*hatamoto*), warlords (*daimyō*), and even members of the Tokugawa clan itself wrote in various 17-syllabet modes on the sly.[13] For instance, the *daimyō* of Hirado domain, Matsuura Seizan (1760–1841), wrote *senryū* under several different pennames, including "Matsuyama," combining the *Matsu* of his family name with an alternate reading of the *zan* (also *san*, "mountain") of his personal name. And Tokugawa Munetake (aka Tayasu Munetake, 1716–1771), first head of the Tayasu branch of the Tokugawa clan, is known to have written *senryū* as well.

13. Hamada, *Edo bungeikō*, 133.

SEVEN

Nevertheless, the efficacy of such pennames as pseudonyms was limited, providing only the barest modicum of temporary protection. Since publishers kept records of authorship, agents of the authoritarian government could, if motivated, find out the identity of just about anyone relatively easily. As a result, there was effectively no such thing as absolute anonymity. For this reason, there are almost no cases of authors in early modern Japan criticizing the government point blank, even under pseudonyms. The result being that most political criticism was couched, oblique, indirect. Hence, while pennames emboldened people, even elites, to write apolitical *senryū*, the feebleness of pseudonyms curtailed direct political satire in *senryū*.

More decisively, authors had a palpable financial incentive to use a penname that could, with minimal effort, be traced back to them. This is because most early modern verses that today are called *senryū* were, in their own day, actually published as part of the contests Makoto Ueda mentioned. These were contests of "versecapping" (*maekuzuke*) in which point-scoring (*tentori*) judges (*tenja*) typically devised 14-syllabet "challenge verses" (*maeku*, literally "fore verses") that were printed on fliers and distributed by field agents, to whom contestants paid a nominal entry fee to submit 17-syllabet "response verses" (*tsukeku*). Winning verses were mass published and circulated widely, in some cases nearly nationwide.

In this respect, early modern versecapping contests were a distant forerunner of the Dai-Ichi Life *sarasen* contest. And not unlike the aforementioned cartoon captioning contest of the *New Yorker* magazine (and that of *Punch* magazine before it), winners could claim bragging rights. Yet the winners of versecapping contests could also earn actual prizes, the most valuable of which might be gold coins or bolts of the finest silk worth tens of thousands of dollars today. Hence, why would contestants pay an entry fee unless there was some way of being contacted should their ship come in? Even when using pennames, in other words, contestants regularly conveyed their real names and contact information to the field agents. It was these field agents who, on behalf of judges, circulated challenge verses and accepted fees along with verses from contestants. Which is why government agents could likewise trace the identity of contestants with minimal effort.

Given the ultimate ineffectiveness of pennames as pseudonyms, then, and the financial incentive of authors to be easily contacted, how are we to understand the widespread use of pennames in *senryū*? In the context of early modern Japanese arts, where artistic-minded individuals habitually assumed a variety of pennames across multiple arts, or even within the same art, I would contend that the penname functioned primarily as *heteronym*, one among many alternate names used to temporarily suspend one's social identity in order to open up a creative artistic space. In this sense, the heteronym is very much like an alter ego, in the parlance of online gaming, an avatar. Whereas the penname as pseudonym was all about concealing identity from others, the penname as heteronym was all about concealing identity from *oneself*.

Broadly speaking, then, the early modern Japanese penname functioned primarily as a heteronym, though may also have been used somewhat perfunctorily as a pseudonym, with the clear understanding that any semblance of protection it afforded was provisional, temporary, feeble. Additionally, however, in the context of the rise of commercial mass publishing during the early modern period, pennames also began acquiring real value as *brand names*. Hence, a penname like "Bashō," which was more heteronym than pseudonym, also became a trademark of sorts associated with a group of writings by one historical person and, by extension, the members of the school bearing his name. There is therefore a tension between the diffusive centrifugal force of the heteronym and the unifying centripetal force of the brand name that must always be kept in mind when considering early modern pennames.

SEVEN

The polyvalence of pennames makes sense in the context of the complex naming practices in early modern Japan. These practices are sometimes glossed over, made to accord with modern Western notions of a single name representing a single individual. However, Japanese name culture is extremely rich, using different kinds of proper names to reflect any changes in social class, age, clan affiliation, rank, and so on over the course of a single person's life. Accordingly, that single individual might assume multiple heteronyms across arts and even within a single artform. Since the nature of literary and artistic production was all about confluence — appropriating concepts, tropes, characters, techniques and so on from one artform into another as well as one artist collaborating with other others — there are very few examples of people limiting themselves to a single artform, even if today an artist is best known for her or his activity in that artform.

Take the case of Manji, a prolific author of *senryū* who, atypically, even composed *senryū* with one of his daughters (who, as it happens, also wrote dirty sexy haiku). The word *manji*, denoting the left-facing "Buddhist swastika" (infamously appropriated then reversed as a sign of Nazism), can also mean "10,000" or "myriad," suggesting the profusion and hoped-for longevity of his verses. Yet today, the name Manji has been almost entirely forgotten, even among serious students of Japanese *senryū*. This is in part because little if any scholarly attention has been paid to *senryū* pennames, since *senryū* are supposedly anonymous. There is also a tendency, in places where name culture is not so complex, to streamline multiple pennames into a single one, for convenience sake (in much the same way that the haiku is said to have derived simply from early modern verse, though in truth the process was far more complex). The *senryū* penname Manji also seems to have been eclipsed by the man's almost ubiquitously-known *nom de plume* in *ukiyo-e*, Katsushika Hokusai (1760 – 1849), whose so-called "Great Wave off Kanagawa" remains iconic of Japan today. Hokusai's sometime writing buddy in *senryū*, it should be mentioned, was none other than his third daughter, Oei (1793–1859), popular as well as scholarly interest in whom has been swelling recently.

Given the ubiquity of heteronyms in early modern Japan, it should come as no surprise that classic haiku poets partook in their use. The most undoubtedly famous name in haiku, Bashō, was itself a heteronym that also eventually became the man's primary brand name. It tags a certain group of writings of a person whose birthname was Matsuo Kinsaku before being changed to the low-ranking samurai name Matsuo Chūemon Munefusa, who also went by the sobriquets Sōbō and Tōsei, and so on.

Moreover, this particular heteronym itself was hardly set in stone; for the reading of its Chinese glyphs was sometimes glossed with the Japanese syllabary in a way that could be read "Haseo" and "Baseo," in addition to Hashō and Bashō. This openness or polyvalence — which also characterizes the playful linked verse (*haikai*) from which both the haiku and *senryū* ultimately derived — is possible because in the historical orthography, the Japanese syllabary (*kana*) glyph for ba could, when written without voice marks (*dakuon*), be pronounced either as *ha* or *ba*. Likewise, the syllabary glyphs for *seo* could be read *seo* or *shō*.

By whatever name, Bashō himself was acutely aware of this polyvalence and deliberately played off of these alternate glosses within his poetry. For instance, there is this verse from *Atsumeku* (1687):

> through countless rimes
> gently this Plantain serves
> as my New Year's pine

> *iku shimo ni / kokorobase o no / matsu kazari*

Although hard to decipher from the Romanized Japanese, the original verse puns on the poet's heteronym. This lightheartedness may surprise those who regard Bashō only as a "serious" poet of supposedly Zen-inspired nature haiku. Yet not only was Bashō more than that—he considered himself to be a master of playful linked verse (haikai) rather than of a modern individual standalone haiku that had yet to be invented—but early modern "haiku" itself was more witty than typically thought of today. Here, the term *matsu kazari* (the "pine decoration" typically put up during the New Year) plays on the poet's family name, "Matsuo." And the phrase *kokorobase o* contains the word *baseo*, which can be read "Bashō." Thus, although the seasonal reference may seem to qualify this verse as a haiku, its overt punning wordplay may also qualify it as a *senryū*.[14] However one categorizes this verse, it is clear that Bashō was having some good-natured self-mocking fun.

Actually, the Bashō heteronym is *itself* self-mocking. As is well known among students of haiku, *bashō* refers to a kind of plantain or, more precisely, Traveler's Palm (*Musa basjoo*). The poet assumed this heteronym in 1680 when, having moved away from the hustle and bustle of down-town Edo to a thatch-roofed retreat in Fukagawa on the outskirts of town, a disciple had gifted him with one or perhaps more of these exotic plants. Native to Okinawa and parts of the Asian mainland, the *bashō* made for a sturdy symbol both of someone or something far flung — Bashō himself originally hailed from Iga Province, some 500 kilometers from Fukagawa and Edo. What is less well known, however, is that, as with most early modern Japanese heteronyms, "Bashō" also suggests humility. Since the leaves of the plant are easily tattered in gusts of wind or rain, the associated sense of frailty or impermanence is a humble acknowledgement of one's tentative place in the universe, poetic or otherwise.

In addition to Bashō, each of the other four Grandmasters of Haiku are known primarily by heteronyms: Yosa (no) Buson

---

14. Granted, the term *senryū* had not been invented in Bashō's day. Nor had the term "haiku" itself, for that matter. At least not as a term signifying an individual standalone verse.

(1716–1784), born Taniguchi Shinshō, was given the childhood name Tora, then assumed a number of heteronyms depending on the artform and period of his life, most notably Yahantei; Issa was born Kobayashi Nobuyuki (1763–1827), took the childhood name Yatarō, and so on; and even Shiki—the modern reformer who is perhaps most responsible for the invented tradition of the modern haiku as a serious form of individual poetry, thereby obscuring its roots and nature in playful linked verse—was a penname of Masaoka Tsunemori (1867–1902), childhood name Tokoronosuke, adolescent name Noboru. The practice of using one or more haiku heteronym began sharply declining at one point, however, especially in the twentieth century, and today, most haiku poets in Japan use their given names.

The conventional wisdom maintaining that *senryū* are anonymous, then, seems to assume that no name, not even a penname, is attached. However, in point of fact, most *senryū* bore pennames. Throughout the early modern period, pennames as heteronyms become brand names, and brand names are the polar opposite of anonymity, in the sense that the former wants a name to be established, whereas the latter does not. The same logic of branding, of making a name famous, informs the pennames of *senryū* and haiku alike, in other words. It might be said that in early modern Japan, in both haiku and *senryū*, the brand name was everything, anonymity nothing.

In closing, it should be stressed that what today are called *senryū* and haiku were both historically published under pennames — "*senryū* pennames" (*ryūgō*) and "haiku pennames" (*haigō*), respectively. The cases of Karai Senryū and Matsuo Bashō are a case in point. These pennames seem to have functioned more as heteronyms (freeing up space for artistic creativity) and brand names (identifying a corpus of writing for commercial purposes) than as pseudonyms (protecting one's real identity, particularly from the government). After all, how can it be that *senryū* pennames imply anonymity, whereas haiku pennames do not? The notion appears to smack of a double standard, or at least an unexamined assumption, as though what really determines anonymity is how lowly or highly these verses are regarded today. For, again, during the early modern period, the government looked askance as haiku as well as *senryū*.

Haiku vs. Senryū

The second reason that the very existence of *senryū* pennames has been so routinely overlooked at best, and misconstrued as evidence of anonymity at worst, may have to do with what might be characterized as a fundamental false dichotomy between haiku and *senryū*. According to this either-or logic, haiku is a serious form of Zen nature poetry, with a season word and cut, composed by a named poet; whereas *senryū* is a playful if nonspiritual form of doggerel about human nature, with no season word or cut, by an anonymous wag. That is to say, haiku is highbrow, *senryū* lowbrow.

Alas, this binary has taken hold to the point that many modern haiku and *senryū* have come to be composed in this manner. Hence, to provide a more accurate picture of the relationship between haiku and *senryū*, one must first overcome the superabundance of poetic examples that unfortunately have come, over the past century in particular, to reify this false dichotomy. While comparisons between haiku and *senryū* can be fruitful, it should not be forgotten that they were never conceived of or composed as polar opposites in their day. For both haiku and *senryū* were merely two among multiple modes of the 17-syllabet verseform and its offshoots associated with playful linked verse (*haikai*), a form of poetic wordplay with complex and often confusing forms and practices that have largely been oversimplified by traditionalist accounts of modern haiku.[15]

---

15. For more on this, see "Introduction" in Kern, xxiii-lxiv.

Such traditionalist accounts assert that the modern haiku emerged directly from the opening verse (*hokku*) of playful linked verse, since the *hokku* mode was less overtly comic than other modes. Nevertheless, the *hokku*—like the *senryū*—was still a playful mode of *haikai*. The binary notion that *all* 17-syllabet verses with seasonal associations and cuts are haiku whereas those without are *senryū* completely neglects the larger context of such playful linked verse, with its multiple modes. For instance, there was the seasonless 17-syllabet verses (*zappai*) that can neither be described as haiku nor *senryū* according to the prevailing binary. And there were "ordinary stanzas" (*hiraku*), which while containing a seasonal association and cut—and therefore are too often clumsily mistaken for *hokku*—nevertheless do not rise to the same lofty heights in tone as the *hokku*. Moreover, some *senryū* have season words and their humor demands the kind of intuitive leap to bridge the disjunction that is the very logic of the cut itself. Hence, both the *hokku* that supposedly gave rise to the modern haiku and the *senryū* were merely two among many different modes of playful linked versification, where the common thread was *playfulness*, rather than the only two modes of 17-syllbet verseform, one serious, the other fatuous.

For another thing, the very notion that Nature and human nature form an ironclad binary is dubious. Do not human beings exist within nature and nature within human beings? What is the point of any mode of poetry, after all, if not to playfully point to ultimate truths about the place of human beings in the natural world in the first place? To the extent that haiku can be said to do as much by focusing on "Nature" and *senryū* on "human nature," it would be wise to refine both concepts beyond the either-or Western Manichean binary, to a more mutually complementary relationship, as with the Eastern notion of yin-yang, where the overlap of or commonality between apparent mutually exclusive opposites is precisely the point. (For this reason, Stephen Addiss's

SEVEN

suggestion that the two exist on a continuum, Nature at one end and human nature on the other, is well taken.) And while it cannot be said that haiku was historically Zen Buddhist poetry (even though a minority of haiku indeed draw on Buddhism), those who view haiku as Buddhist would be hard pressed to explain the binary thinking when Buddhism itself posits the transcendence of mere binaries.[16]

Simply put, then, the thinking that the haiku is highbrow whereas the *senryū* is lowbrow suffers from the misleading either-or logic of the haiku versus *senryū* dialectic without an adequate contextualization of these modes in the larger world of playful linked verse. This dialectic also smacks of an elitism—as though only haiku are worth taking credit for—that goes against the very grain of the spirit of haiku as well as the egalitarianism of playful linked verse, which admitted players from any class, background, and gender. In their day, both haiku and *senryū* were considered lowbrow, certainly versus the highbrow 31-syllabet *tanka* or *waka*.

The rise of commercial mass woodblock-printing in the seventeenth century naturally increased the tendency toward commer-cialism in the arts. It was not long before artists—and publishers—realized that using and attaching a single heteronym to a corpus of artistic or literary works as a kind of brand name could help stimulate interest and thus consumption. Hence, the heteronym as brand name Bashō came to prevail. Amateur authors

---

16. All this is not to inadvertently pose a false binary between East and West, by the way. Phenomenology, deconstruction, poststructuralism, and many other systems of thought and philosophies in the West, including quantum physics (as with the Heisenberg Uncertainty Principle if not Einstein's Theory of Relativity itself), for instance, have been to some degree deeply influenced by the non-binary thinking of Buddhism. In my opinion, this particular encounter between Eastern and Western philosophy may well represent, a bit paradoxically, one of the least commented upon but most profound intellectual developments over the past half millennium. For more on this subject, see, for instance, Ramirez-Christensen.

of today's *sarasen*, by contrast, since they are not constructing a body of works for sale attached to a brand name, can be more nimble with their heteronyms or pseudonyms. Indeed, comparing the heteronyms associated with classical *senryū* with those of *sarasen*, we see something new emerging: although not always the case, the *sarasen* heteronym has become increasingly exploited as a means of adding information to a verse, as a way of overcoming the 17-syllabet limitations of the verseform. Because of the nimbleness of the *sarasen* heteronym, and in some cases pseudonym, it can be used to confirm a likely reading or augment the verse, or even add necessary information without which the verse would lack some or even any clarity.

True, some *sarasen* poets write multiple verses under the same heteronym. A case in point is one Takane no Bara, three of whose verses are translated herein. So it is not the case that all heteronyms are individuated each and every time. Yet most of the time, these heteronyms are attached to a single *sarasen* in a way that reveals something interesting or even essential about the content of the verse. Simply put, pennames have evolved in a fundamental way that has provided *sarasen* with an additional resource that early modern *senryū* appear not to have had at their disposal, at least so far as the present preliminary study suggests.

Naming Names

Generally speaking, the transition in Japan from early modern dictatorship to modern democracy has allowed the arts to express sociopolitical criticism more directly. Still, the change from indirectness in early modern *senryū* to directness in modern *sarasen* is nothing if not conspicuous. Consider the following three early modern verses that pushed the envelope perhaps as far as it could reasonably have been pushed at the time:

SEVEN

> one's shadow
> reaching the ceiling of rank
> breaks bad!
>
> *tenjō e / tsukaete / magaru / kageboshi*

This *senryū*, written under the penname Gosei, was published in 1788, though like the best modern *sarasen*, its point about the hypocrisy of those lording it over others could well apply to government corruption today. There is a certain universality to the best classic *senryū* and *sarasen* that transcend the particulars of their time and place, in other words.

Here is another verse, a swipe at the entire samurai class:

> rustic samurai!
> muckin' around now more in paddies
> than with poetry
>
> *inaka bushi / ima wa shi yori mo / ta o tsukuri*

The verse was published in *Marumaru chinbun* in 1878 (a year after the magazine began publication). With the fall of the Tokugawa shogunate in 1868, members of the samurai class had had no recourse but to turn to lower occupations, even returning to the provinces to take up farming. The fiercely proud and learned samurai are derided in the verse — or ironically self-mocked, if the author him- or herself was a samurai? — by the double meanings of *inaka* as "uncultured" and "provincial," and of *tsukuri* as "composing" poetry as well as "tilling" the fields.

Although these two verses are generalized, here is another classic *senryū* that is often said to have had targeted a particular member of the Japanese government:

> the bureaucrat's tot
> learns about grabby-grabby
> an awful lot!
>
> *yakunin no / ko wa niginigi o / yoku oboe*

This verse, by an unnamed author, was published in the inaugural volume of *Yanagidaru* (1765). Lightness of tone and punning wordplay accentuate the biting sarcasm here. *Yoku*, "frequently" or "well," has homonyms in "greed" and "succeeding (generation)." *Niginigi*, "clench hold of" in children's parlance, calls to mind an infant reflexively grasping an object — perhaps the finger of a parent, seemingly out of affection. In the case of a government official, by contrast, selfish "bribe taking" or even "power *grabbing*" may be insinuated.

Now, this particular satire is often read as having been aimed at Tanuma Okitsugu (1719–88), reputedly the most corrupt public figure of the period. However, Tanuma began serving as senior counsellor (*rōjū*) to the shogun only in 1767, two years *after* publication of this verse in 1765. In a society organized according to a hereditary class system, the greater social issue no doubt was generational nepotism.

In fact, for all intents and purposes, there were no authors or poets in early modern Japan who transgressed the rules against direct mention of government officials — although there was one storyteller who unwittingly transgressed.[17] If anything, that one

17. The best known if not only person to run afoul of the authorities for having made direct mention of an official was reputedly oral storyteller (*kōdanshi*) Baba Bunkō (ca. 1718-1759). Working in the Asakusa Temple area of Edo (now Tokyo), Bunkō told war stories, human interest tales, reports of the latest rumors, and gossip about public officials — even to the point, apparently, of mentioning the ninth Tokugawea shogun, Ieshige (1712–1761), by name. In one of his spiels, Bunkō also purportedly protested *daimyō* Kanamori Yorikane's (1713–1763) treatment of peasants in Gujō domain (present-day Gifu). Unbeknownst to Bunkō, someone in the audience transcribed and published Bunkō's talk under

case suggests both the inadequacy of pennames as pseudonyms and the resultant chilling effect on direct political criticism within popular works. In this sense, the totalitarian regime was alarmingly successful. No such instances of anything like this incident appear, to the best of my knowledge, anywhere in the annals of early modern *senryū*. This is not to say that something could come to light in the future, however. At the time of this writing, at least, it seems safe to say that classic socio-politically charged *senryū*, in keeping with general tendencies during the day, never overtly named names. As we shall see, such cannot be said for some of contemporary *sarasen*, where names are indeed named as part of sharp political satire, even the names of prime ministers.

Sketchy Satire

This brings us to the last of the three major points. Although the political satire of early modern *senryū* was never direct, the modern *sarasen* not only can be direct, it moreover has become arguably the major form of political satire today, even more so than the editorial cartoon. Whereas one of the most visible forms of such criticism, the editorial cartoon, has seemed to shrink away from direct satire, *sarasen* has stepped up as arguably the major form of political satire today. This may be because professional cartoonists have a brand name to protect, as do the newspapers which have traditionally run such cartoons. *Sarasen* using heteronyms, by contrast, have no such reputation to maintain, and therefore can claim far more latitude for themselves. Moreover, Japanese media tend to exercise extreme sensitivity with respect to victims of major national traumas. The contrast between the circumspectness of mainstream cartoons and the frankness of *sarasen* is especially apparent in such cases.

---

his penname as a short chapbook. Not long after this chapbook reached the authorities, Bunkō was dragged before a court and summarily executed. For more on this incident, see Farge.

To understand this situation, it may be useful to situate early modern *senryū* and modern *sarasen* in the larger historical context of sociopolitical satire in the literary and visual arts in Japan. Sociopolitical satire has a long, rich tradition in Japan, even setting aside the school of thought that maintains that all art and literature can be said to have a political cast.

Generally speaking, one finds many early classics of Japanese literature siding with this or that faction, or at least its representative, at the imperial court, with winners and looser clearly delineated. In a sense, *Genji monogatari* (The Tale of Genji, ca. 1000), widely hailed as the world's first great "novel" of interiority or psychological depth, covers the progeny of a losing faction at court, and therefore can be read, in the main, as a kind of oblique criticism of aristocratic court life, even as the protagonist for much of the tale, the Shining Prince Genji aspires to be accepted by that very world. Political divisions, exile, intrigue, marriage politics, and romantic entanglements galore form the stuff of the story. In the great imperial collections of poetry, those whom the powers that be favored often had their poems included, whereas the converse cannot always said to be true. To take perhaps the most famous example, the great general Taira no Tadanori (1144–1184), brother of the Taira clan leader Taira no Kiyomori (1118–1181), was on the losing side of the Genpei War (1180–1185) between the Taira and Minamoto (or Genji) clans. As a result, Tadanori could not have his poems openly included in the imperial collection of the winning side, the *Senzai Wakashū* (Collection of a Thousand Years, 1187). Nevertheless, compiler Fujiwara no Shunzei (1114–1204) decided to include one of Tadanori's poems anyway, albeit under the anonym *Yomihito Shirazu* (Poet Unknown).

The field of visual caricature likewise has a venerable history in Japan, beginning, perhaps, with the cartoon-like caricatures scribbled, as early as the eighth century, under the eaves of Hōryūji in Nara (the same temple that figures along with persimmon eating in a famous

SEVEN

verse by Shiki, by the way). One of the earliest if most famous extant manuscripts of caricature in Japan is no doubt the so-called "Toba pictures" (*tobae*), a set of celebrated comic scrolls, regularly attributed to the late Heian-period monk Toba Sōjō (1053–1140), entitled *Chōjū giga* (Frolicking Critters, ca. late 12th early 13th c.), that depict animals in human activities, such as reciting sutras and sumo wrestling. This style of caricature somehow continued into the Edo period. These hastily sketched comics, which used exaggeration and gesture to attain their expressiveness, featured zany, homunculus little human beings with round heads, squinty eyes, and triangles for noses. Many such books were published in the eighteenth century.[18] The Toba cartoon influenced the Shijō and Nanga Schools most directly, though it also is evident in the works of Hokusai, illustrations in madcap poetry (*kyōka*) books, and elsewhere.

The works of Jichosai, one of the great *tobae* cartoonists of the late eighteenth and early nineteenth centuries, include *Ehon kototsugai* (Picturebook of Counterparts; published by Kawachiya Kihei in Osaka in 1805) and *Tobae Ōgi no mato* (Fan Targets, Toba Cartoon-style, 1790).

The merging of literary and visual caricature was the lifeblood of woodblock-printed comic books (*kusazōshi*) and other forms of so-called "frivolous literature" (*gesaku*) during the Edo period. So much so that *senryū* was often referred to as "frivolous verse" (*zareku*), where the "frivolous" (*zare*) was written with the same Chinese glyph as the "frivolous" (*ge*) of "frivolous literature" (*gesaku*). Bashō himself even seems to have used the term "fooling around verse" (*zaretaruku*) to refer to what might today be recognized as *senryū*.[19]

---

18. For more on this, see Shimizu.
19. Quoted in Sanzō shi. In Yamashita, 234.

When Western editorial cartoons began seeping into Japan, Japanese artists seemed to merge the visual and literary caricature (of things such as *tobae* and other forms of caricature within *gesaku*) with Western artistic and journalistic techniques. Western influence began with Charles Wirgman's *The Japan Punch* (1862–1887) and continued in homemade Japanese humor magazines, such as *Nipponichi* and *Marumaru chinbun*. Some of the *senryū* herein originally appeared in the latter. One of the pivotal figures in moving newspaper caricature toward modern Western artistic and journalistic techniques was Kitazawa Rakuten (1876–1955). This was a long process, one that has begun to be studied by Peter Duus, Ron Stewart, and others. The one feature, however, that most closely unites *gesaku*, *senryū* (whether classic or modern), and Western political cartoons is the exposé (*ana o ugashi*, literally "excavating a loophole," or *ugachi* for short). The exposé was central to *gesaku* and, specifically, a kind of woodblock-printed comicbook (*kusazōshi*) known as the *kibyōshi* (yellow covers). In fact, writer-artists like Koikawa Harumachi, Santō Kyōden, and Shikitei Sanba were all ultimately held to task for their activities in this genre, although none of them executed.

Particularly over the past decade or two, however, there has been a precipitous decline in the grand tradition of Japanese political cartooning in print. Although part of the reason for this no doubt has to do with how much of this energy has moved online, the major newspapers, which have an online presence as well as one in print, have still been shying away from political cartoons by professionals. In part, this is because the media environment in Japan itself has been changing radically over the past decade or two. As Patrick W. Galbraith and Jason G. Karlin suggest in "Introduction: At the Crossroads of Media Convergence in Japan":

> Whereas newspapers — Japan has the highest circulation in the world — and television — Japanese watch and trust it more than many others in the world — could once count on being able

SEVEN

> to filter information and set the terms of national discussion, social media has led to an explosive proliferation of channels of communication. This is especially notable after the natural and nuclear disasters that shook Japan on March 11, 2011, which did much to foster skepticism of the mainstream media and its perceived alliance with the state, as well as popularize social media as an alternative source of information (2).

Hence, it may well be that sociopolitical satire has moved online, specifically social media, from mainstream publi-cations.

Scholar Ron Stewart has investigated political cartoons in the three largest newspapers in Japan (*Yomiuri*, *Asahi*, and *Mainichi*) devoted to the triple disaster in Fukushima of the earthquake, tsunami, and nuclear meltdown on March 11, 2011. Stewart found that the newspapers were collectively irresponsive on 3-11 (as the triple disaster is referred to in Japan, echoing the American 9-11), issuing only "bland calls for unity and for support for the government" (187). And even then, it was too little too late. Generally speaking, Stewart feels that the most biting satire in cartoons is to be found "online" and in less mainstream magazines. One wonders if that temporary suspension of cartoons has not led to a further erosion of political cartooning in Japan, since the three major print newspapers have all but permanently suspended their cartoon programs, leaving politically inflected *sarasen* as the last bastion of such critical public discourse.

Indeed, setting aside the proliferation of online cartooning in Japan, the major form of sociopolitical satire within mainstream media, especially print, now appears to be the *sarasen*. This is not to say *sarasen* is the major form of sociopolitical satire today in all media and platforms, for one would need to compare *sarasen* satire to that in television, movies, anime, online manga, online political cartoons unaffiliated with the major print newspapers, and so on, a project that will have to remain for someone else to take up.

Yet spite of the decline of newspaper cartooning, there is no dearth of amateur *senryū*. How is this possible? Major Japanese newspapers have, since their beginnings in the late nineteenth century, dedicated weekly columns to various kinds of haiku and *senryū* sent in by readers. It was only natural for modern journalism to draw on the exposé that was so foundational to early modern frivolous literature (*gesaku*). The following *senryū*, published in the inaugural issue of the socio-political satirical magazine *Marumaru chinbun* (1877), comments on the modern method that newspapers (*shinbun*) favor in "exposing the loopholes" (*ana o hori*) of the "floating world" of popular culture:

> floating world —
> newspapers unearth its loopholes
> with the pen!
>
> *shinbun wa / fude de ukiyo no / ana o hori*[20]

Although modern Western-style moveable-type newspapers and magazines had begun appearing in Japan during the second half of the nineteenth century, there had already been a century-long history of woodblock-printed scandal sheets (*kawaraban*), gossip rags (*yomiuri*), and comic literature that exalted the exposé.

Marumaru chinbun is often best remembered today for its pioneering political cartoons. Yet these were just one part of its editorial profile. Politically pointed *senryū*, whether sent in by readers or penned by staff, abounded on the topics of the day, from Western-style enlightenment to women's suffrage:

---

20. Verses from *Marumaru chinbun* were reprinted without attribution in Yamamoto. Whether this means the verses were published anonymously or not, however, will remain unclear until the actual issues of *Marumaru chinbun* can be consulted.

SEVEN

> shining the light
> on social enlightenment —
> electric lamps!
>
> *bunmei no / hikari wa denki- / tō de shire*

In *Marumaru chinbun* (1889). Japanese people of the Meiji period read about modern Western-style "civilization" (*bunmei*, "lettered brightness") literally by the very "electric lighting" (*denkitō*, an oldfangled word for *dentō*) that was part of that civilization.

> civilized skies
> stretching out into writing
> gone sideways
>
> *bunmei no / sora yokomoji ni / wataru nari*

In *Marumaru chinbun* (1889).

> even love letters
> by civilized young ladies
> in block style!
>
> *bunmei no / musume wa fumi mo / kaisho nari*

In *Marumaru chinbun* (1879). *Kaisho*, the block style of handwriting associated with the West, can also mean "resourcefulness."

> beefsteak
> as well as Western languages —
> just a soupçon!
>
> *bifuteki to / yōgo mo sukoshi / kuikajiri*

In *Marumaru chinbun* (1891). *Kuikajiri* means both a 'nibble' of food and a 'smattering' of knowledge. The Japanese term *bifuteki*, "beefsteak," entered the language as a loan word from the French *bifteck*.

> insufferable
> even for politicians—
> women's suffrage!

seijika mo / komaru nyōbo no / jiyūshugi

In *Chōchōshi koji tsuizen* (1889). Although the women's rights movement began in Japan after the Meiji Restoration, women would not be granted the right to vote until after the Second World War.

> socialism:
> nothing up and running
> except taverns!

shakaishugi / izakaya bakari / aruite i

And even then, the conversations no doubt consist primarily of griping about socialism. This *senryū*, by Sakai Kuraki, appeared in his collection *Senryū kurakiten* (1904) rather than in a newspaper. Even as this verse is explicitly political, in that it deals with political movements and parties, it is not aimed at any one politician in particular.

Recent Sarasen: From Bitter Armageddon to Coronapocalypse

In modern and contemporary Japan, amateur *senryū* has continued to be published in newspapers and magazines. Within this outpouring of comic verse, a special kind of *senryū* emerged purportedly championing the view of the average citizen as exemplified by the male salaried employee of Japanese companies.

SEVEN

In his essay on the subject, Gardner included several salaryman *senryū* related to Aum Shin Rikyō, the doomsday cult responsible for the lethal 1995 sarin gas attack on the Tokyo subway. It is therefore fitting that we pick up where Gardner left off, commencing our survey of *sarasen* with one about the execution of the cult's leader, Asahara Shōkō, years later, in July 2018:

> Asahara—
> at last reaping his own bitter
> Armageddon

> *Asahara ya / shishite harumage / haru daikon*[21]

The original Japanese verse contains sardonic wordplay that, like so many *sarasen* (and early modern *senryū* alike), is challenging to render in English translation: Asahara, literally "hemp field," calls to mind the "spring" (*haru*) in both the Japanese word for the apocalypse (*harumage*) and in "spring radishes" (*haru daikon*), a proverbial expression for reaping the harvest that one sows. Significantly, this verse defies the haiku vs. *senryū* binary, for on the one hand, the presence of a seasonal association (spring) and cutting word (the *ya* ending the first phrase) suggests haiku, whereas the sardonic wordplay clearly places the verse in the realm of *senryū*. Either way, much like the editorial or political cartoon, the best *sarasen* serve as exposé, the most relevant examples irresistibly capturing the national zeitgeist.

In addition to packing a wallop, *sarasen* can do so quickly, being published within a day or two of a contemporary event. This makes them ever so slightly more nimble than political cartoons, which often lag several more days behind the events they address. Plus, *senryū* take up less print space than cartoons. In the wake of the March 2011 earthquake, tsunami, and nuclear meltdown

---

21. https://blog.goo.ne.jp/nichikon1/e/8359e1eb0abdc04bda34f102764654b4. Accessed December 2020.

in Fukushima (some 300 km north of Tokyo) that claimed some 18,000 lives, Japan's major newspapers temporarily suspended their editorial cartoons. Ostensibly, this was self-censorship out of consideration for those who had lost loved ones. Some newspapers actually claimed with a straight face — as though critical editorial cartoons provide no useful function to society — that there was simply too much important news about Fukushima to squander any space on cartoons about Fukushima. Still, such claims failed to account for why these same newspapers continued to run their daily *apolitical* cartoon strips. Hence, newspapers treated the triple disaster as though merely writing about it was radioactive.

There are Japanese graphic novels (*manga*) on Fukushima, to be sure. One powerful example is *Ichi Efu* (2014), written by an amateur artist under the pseudonym Tatsuta Kazuto, a volunteer who quickly became outraged about Tokyo Electric and Power Company's (TEPCO) cover-up of the full extent of the disaster. Kyō Machiko's *Mitsuami no kamisama* (Gods in Pigtails, 2013) has its own brand of pushback, though it is so gentle, one shudders to call it political satire in the first place. It's more like a cute but sad lament for the everyday items lost in the disaster or abandoned in the aftermath by their human users. In this respect, the work seems to be a modern incarnation of the folk belief in "object goblins" (*tsukumogami*) — that is, the spirits of inanimate objects. Still, this work has taken several years to unfold. *Sarasen*, by comparison, can be composed and published and absorbed almost instantaneously.

Fortunately, *sarasen* sent in by readers in the wake of the triple disaster have survived the cuts. This means that the *sarasen* has effectively become the major vehicle in mainstream media for average people to criticize the mishandling of the nuclear plant meltdown by the Japanese government as well as TEPCO:

> radiation leaks —
> if only we'd been notified
> I wouldn't have cancer

> *kōgai more / shirasete kureterya / gan narazu*

Although no names are named, there can be little mistake as to the intended targets of this verse ("3.11 Hinansha Senryū" no. 289, December 2016), by the poignantly named Toki Sudeni Ososhi (Suddenly Already Too Late).

> blindly believing
> the official announcements —
> my own idiocy!

> *kuni no shiji / shinjita washi ga / baka deshita*

By Yori Senryō no Takai Kata e Nigeteshimatta (Someone Who Fled from a Place with High Radiation; "3.11 Hinansha Senryū" no. 288, September 2016).

> the real problem
> is less technology
> than lack of trust

> *mondai wa / kagaku dewanaku / shin'yōdo*

The lack of trust here refers to the government's mishandling of some catastrophe: the triple disaster, the novel coronavirus pandemic, the Olympics, take your pick. This was one of the only *sarasen* I surveyed for the present article that was published anonymously ("Minna de Seiji Senryū," no. 1126, April 2021).

> what sort of nation
> makes its people tremble whenever
> power plants rumble?
>
> *yureru tabi / genpatsu harahara / nante kuni*

By Konna Jishin Taikoku ni 54 Ki (54 Nuclear Plants in This Nation Leading in Earthquakes). This penname was most likely coined around the time of the triple disaster, when there were 54 power plants in Japan (even though the verse was published in November 2016, "3.11 Hinansha Senryū," no. 305). Since then, 21 of those plants have been decommissioned. Of the 33 remaining, only 9 are actually functioning (at least as of March 2021).[22]

Some *sarasen* transcend indignation, addressing the heartbreaking human tragedy, as with this rather breathless verse, expressing genuine sympathy for the survivors and, by extension, the victims:

> Fukushima folks . . .
> their poems . . . a certain tightness
> in the chest
>
> *fukushima no / hito, yomu poemu / munagurushi*

This moving verse ("3.11 Hinansha Senryū," no. 313, November 2016), by Nando Naita Ka Wakaranai (Don't Know How Many Times I've Wept), closes the gap between the humor of many sociopolitical sarasen and the bitterness that so often resides deeper down, at their very core. The use of the English loanword for poem (poemu) somehow makes Fukushima folks seem more cosmopolitan, more sophisticated.

---

22. https://www.nippon.com/ja/japan-data/h00967/?fbclid=IwAR1MaV7AJFZfP3ohKudcZIW5dGiAtiiNX_qUCPoLKH2_9QVcmY4A_FWNZqw. Accessed March 2021.

Another such *sarasen*:

> my hometown
> and the ocean, both lost —
> nuclear power

furusato mo / umi mo ushinau / genshiryoku

By Takane no Bara (High-peak Rosebush; "Minna de Seiji Senryū," no. 1126, April 2021).

Others *sarasen* excavate hidden contradictions in social myths, as with this verse by Wasurenbō (Absentminded), which placed 11th in the 2020 contest:

> ecofriendly?
> this rapid proliferation
> of reusable bags

eko na no ka / dondon fueru / maibakku

Sarasen's Trump Card

The momentary, topical nature of many *sarasen* allows them to reach people with a kind of direct urgency. On the other hand, the topicality more often than not requires a bit of historical excavation. Then again, the same is often true of political cartoons. Like the best of these, the best political *sarasen* speak to the moment in a way that at the time seems to transcend the moment, to a realm of universal truths. Only those truths may not be accessible a few years later, after the specifics of that particular moment have been all but forgotten.

The wordplay in the following verse, which was immediately appreciable when it was written, superficially suggests that even cultural icons have been adversely affected by a certain American president:

> once upon a time
> Donald was the name of a duck
> but now, a mad dog!
>
> *donarudo wa / mukashi ahiru de / ima kyōken*

Written by Suginami Ojisan (Uncle from Suginami) long before said president smeared Omarosa Manigault Newman, or incited the January 6 insurrection, this verse appeared in January 2017 ("Marusen"), when Trump was inexplicably threatening to slap a tariff on Toyota. Headquartered in Japan, one of the United States' major allies and trading partners, Toyota is nevertheless a multinational corporation, with factories in America. Thus, this *sarasen* more sharply strikes at the irrationality of Trump's trade wars, which seem likely to backfire, hurting American exports far beyond Disney characters.

Some *sarasen* authors have noted the irony that Trump's pursuing isolationist anti-Muslim policies would make America precisely the kind of "closed nation" that Japan had supposedly become during the Tokugawa period:

> shut-ins
> who are anti-Muslim:
> a closed nation
>
> *hikikomori / isuramu dame to / sakoku suru*

Furthermore, the irony of the verse ("Marusen" January 2017) is deepened by how its author, Hanka Monosan (Halfway Human), deploys the term *hikikomari*, referring to a social misfit who stays at home all the time and is unfortunately associated with contemporary Japan. The joke here is that although Japan had once shut itself off from the world according to a policy of national isolation, it is now America that has effectively become isolationist.

Some *sarasen* take a swipe at the then-president's very name (something we will find in *sarasen* about Japanese politicians as well):

> with a name like Trump
> one can hardly maintain
> a pokerface
>
> *na wa toranpu / pōkāfeisu / dekinu hito*

The humor of this verse ("Marusen" January 2017), also by Suginami Ojisan (Uncle from Suginami), may come across slightly less poorly in the original, since the Japanese term for playing cards is *toranpu* ("trump").

For those Japanese who struggle to understand how America — a land of immigrants from diverse racial as well as cultural backgrounds — could elect a president given to such protectionism and xenophobia, if not outright racism, there's this one, which goes right to the heart of the matter, if not the jugular:

> long story short:
> he wants to make America
> white again
>
> *yōsuru ni / hakujin koku ni / shitain da*

By Bungaraya-san. ("Marusen" February 2017).

Actually, *sarasen* about Trump seem to outstrip even the volume of his remarks on Twitter, most of which seemed to dig him into deeper and deeper trouble (before he was eventually banned):

> every single Tweet:
> one more milestone on the road
> to Russiagate!
>
> *tsuiito wa /roshiamon e no / ichirizuka*

By Ichiyu Ichiyu ("Marusen" June 2017).[23] Here, *roshiamon* deviates from the typical Japanese term for Russiagate (*roshiageeto*), thereby calling to mind "Rashōmon," the classic film by director Kurosawa Akira (1910–1998) that not only is known for its exploration of the radical subjectivity of truth, but also as a meditation on egocentrism and human nature itself. In his screenplay, Kurosawa adapted two earlier short stories by author Akutagawa Ryūnosuke (1892–1927), *Yabu no naka* and *Rashōmon* (themselves adaptations of even earlier stories), the former being about radical subjectivity, the latter about the main gate to the capital during Japan's medieval civil wars — a gate that in the story was possessed in its upper echelons by a demonic presence.

> Donald Trump's yap:
> there should be a law against
> its noise pollution!
>
> *toranpu no / kuchi e sōon / kiseihō*

Kisei, "prohibition," also puns on "bizarre voice." By Masaki ("Tamura Akiko's Senryū Blog," November 2016).

Yet lest anyone in Japan develop a superiority complex — and true to the irreverence that marks so many *sarasen* (and early modern *senryū*), there is this verse by Sakiji (like the verse above, on "Tamura Akiko's Senryū Blog," November 2016):

---

23. This penname is written with the Chinese characters for 1-2-1-2 and so could be read in a variety of ways (e.g. Ichiji Ichiji, Ichini ichini, Ichiji Katsuji, Ichiji Kazuji, etc). However, one Twitter user interested in *senryū* who writes his name this way glosses it "Ichiyu Ichiyu."

SEVEN

> we Japanese
> have also had our fair share
> of foulmouthed pols
>
> *kuchi no warui / seijika nihon / nimo ita ne*

Speaking of whom:

> Isn't that dandy!
> Mr. Trump's also putting
> America first
>
> *Aa, yokatta! / toranpu-san mo / amerika daiichi de*

By Tokumei-san (Mr. Anonymous) ("Marusen" January 2017). The insinuation being that Japanese politicians have kissed America's ass long and hard.

The following *sarasen* would be all but incomprehensible were it not for three clues: the stated topic of "Trump," the date of publication, and the author's penname:

> no chance of winning
> and shouldn't be contesting
> nevertheless . . .
>
> *kachime nai / kenka o shinai / hazu nanoni*

The reading and meaning of the penname to this verse is slightly ambiguous. One rendering may be "Kawazu Bunka," literally "Frog Letters Under," suggesting literature in the wake of Bashō's celebrated poem about the frog jumping into an old pond. However, given that the verse was posted on November 17, 2020 ("Marusen"), at a moment when Trump was conspicuously refusing to concede the election to President Elect Joe Biden, the name should probably be read as "Kaeru Monka" (Hell No, I Won't Go!). This plays off a homonym of *kaeru* as "return" or "change," and the colloquial phrase *monka*, "no way am I going to.. . . ." In which case the name would suggest "Like Hell am I going to Change!" or, even more to the point, "Hell no, Trump won't leave (the White House)!"[24]

"Abesurd" Masks and Prime Minister Dud

Historically, the early modern *senryū* engaged in sociopolitical satire, as we have seen, though political topics were almost always treated with kid gloves, certainly not mentioning any politicians point blank. How slowly times have changed. Most political *sarasen* today pull their punches, too. Yet for the first time in Japanese history, perhaps, some do not. Take the case of sarasen aimed squarely at politicians, particularly former Prime Minister Abe Shinzo and current Prime Minister (at the time of this writing) Suga Yoshihide.

Abe Shinzo (b. 1954), a far right-wing politician affiliated with the long-ruling Liberal Democratic Party and who served as Prime Minister longer than anybody else in modern Japanese history, is known for his conservative fiscal policies (dubbed "Abenomics"), his desire to reform Article 9 of the Japanese constitution (forbidding Japan from keeping let alone using nuclear weapons), and, equally troublingly to his critics, his extreme revisionist views on sensitive international topics. Most conspicuously, perhaps, Abe's view that the Japanese government played no role whatsoever during the Pacific War in recruiting the euphemistically termed "comfort women" (*ianfu*) — in reality, forced sexual slaves—has been roundly condemned by almost all historians of the issue.

---

24. Alternatively, the first two characters could be the family name Abun, and the last two characters could be the first name Hodatsushi, though the overlapping character would preclude both of these names being read that way at the same time.

SEVEN

Many average Japanese were skeptical of Abe's politics, too. Consider the following *sarasen* that takes sarcastic aim at the putative objectivity of the so-called "Japan Conference" (*Nippon kaigi*), consisting of Abe and other far righters who minimize or even outright deny accounts of the Japanese Rape of Nanking as exaggerated:

> the Japan Conference —
> purely an apolitical bunch
> of old fools
>
> *Nippon kaigi / tada nonpori no /baka rōjin*

By Nankai Pōkusu, "Southsea Porks," punning on "Southsea Hawks" (Nankai Hōkusu), the name of a professional baseball team in Fukuoka ("Senryūjin" no. 36005, August 2018).[25]

More recently, innumerable *sarasen* ridiculed Abe's infamously poor response to the coronavirus pandemic, the centerpiece of which was sending two washable cloth masks to every household in Japan, regardless of the number of occupants. A house with eight members, say, received the same two masks as a house with a single member. Making matters worse, the masks were miniscule and ridiculous looking. Punsters soon transformed the "Abe mask" (*Abe no masuku*), as it was widely termed, into the "idiot mask" (*aho no masuku*):

> Abe-surd mask:
> too damn embarrassing
> to be worn!
>
> *aho no masuku / hazukashikutte / tsukaenai*

By Etchan ("Minna de Seiji Senryū," no. 1010, May 2020).

25. http://www.senryunin.com/keyword.php?sSenryu=true&sYomibito=true&kword=%E6%97%A5%E6%9C%AC%E4%BC%9A%E8%AD%B0.

> Grand Prize:
> an idiotic Abe mask
> as suspected
>
> *taishō wa / aho no masuku to / omotteta*

By Soyogu (Flutter; "Minna de Seiji Senryū," no. 1051, Dec 2020).

The anemic response of the Japanese government's overall response to the pandemic has occasioned more than one *cri de cœur*:

> enough, already!
> with the lies and deceitfulness
> and heresy!
>
> *tsukareru yo / uso to gomakashi / gedō kana*

By Koki Jīsan (70ish Gramps; "Minna de Seiji Senryū," no. 1035, August 2020). "Heresy" here renders *gedō*, literally "outside ways," a Buddhist term for *tirthika*, or non-Buddhist teachings, meaning any kind of heterodoxy. Yet *gedō* is more often used popularly in Japan as a pejorative for general fiendishness or devilry.

Problems with the vaccine rollout during the Covid-19 pandemic, testing kit shortages, and a higher rate of deadly side effects (relative to other countries) among the lucky few who have been able to get vaccinated in the first place have fueled more than one hopeless, bitter verse, as with this one, written after Abe was out of office:

> c'mon, already!
> get this bloody virus
> under control!
>
> *korona koso / andā kontorōru / shitekure yo*

By Konna Hitotachi (These People!; "Minna de Seiji Senryū," no. 1116, April 2021). The force of using the English loan word "under control" (andā kontorōru) suggests the extremes to which the poet wants the Japanese government to go.

> Astra vaccine —
> be my guest for the first shot,
> politicians!
>
> *asutoro no / senkō sesshu wa / seijika de*

This verse, submitted by the aptly self-styled Yogensha (Prophesizer) in February 2021 ("Minna de Seiji Senryū," no.1094), preceded the scaling back of the Astra Zeneca vaccination in April 2021 due to safety concerns, meaning complications including death.

No wonder the following verse, which has the feel of a motto gone horribly awry:

> no testing
> no vaccination
> no hope
>
> *kensa nashi / wakuchin nashi de / kibō nashi*

By one Akumu no Suka Seiken (Nightmarish Sucky Administration; "Minna de Seiji Senryū," no. 1111, April 2021).

And:

> enough is enough!
> those who prop up this letdown
> piss me off!
>
> *genkai da / suka o katsuida / hai ni hara ga tatsu*

Korona ni Obieru Sugomoru Okina (Old Man Roosting in Fear of Corona; "Minna de Seiji Senryū," no. 1081, January 2021).

The operative word in the pseudonym of the previous verse, and in the present verse, is *suka*, "letdown," or "failure, flop, washout," etc. This has become something of a standard if strained pun on the family name of Prime Minister Suga Yoshihide (b. 1948).[26] A career bureaucrat who has held various positions with the Liberal Democratic Party under Abe, Suga became Prime Minister himself in September 2020. Suga famously appeared on camera to publicly unveil the new imperial name of the Reiwa era (which began in May 2019). The beginning of his rule was also just in time for the deepening of the coronavirus pandemic in Japan. Like Abe's, Suga's response has been widely criticized as indecisive. Accordingly, his approval ratings, which had approached 75% when he first assumed office, tanked over 30% within a few months, to just over 40%. In an online article for financial magazine *Toyo Keizai*, political journalist Hiroshi Izumi asked pointedly: "When will Prime Minister Suga, the author of a book *Resolution of a Politician*, whose motto is 'Where there is a will there is a way,' take decisive action?"[27]

Other nicknames for Suga have been circulating in social media and *sarasen*, as with "Sugalin" (*sugarin* in Japanese), a portmanteau mixing "Suga" and "Stalin," insinuating that the Japanese Prime Minister has the same authoritarian tendencies — and little tolerance for dissent — as the murderous Soviet leader. Yet the most prevalent association of *suka*, in the context of the lottery, is a losing ticket, or "dud." Hence, there are innumerable *sarasen* poking fun at PM Sucky or PM Dud. Fevers have been running high over the Japanese government's handling — or, judging by the criticism, mishandling — of the coronavirus pandemic:

---

26. As most educated Japanese are aware, classical Japanese sometimes suspended the diacritical marks (*dakuon*) that could, for instance, turn *k* sounds into *g* sounds. In this way, the word *suka* can be read as either *suka* or *suga*.
27. Quoted in Yamaguchi. Suga's motto, in Japanese, is *ishi areba michi ari*.

SEVEN

> Prime Minister Dud —
> a perfectly fitting phrase
> for a dud ticket
>
> *suka sōri / suka to wa hazure nari / iietemyō*

By Takane no Bara (High-peak Rosebush; "Minna de Seiji Senryū," no. 1083, January 2021).

> teleshopping —
> more spunk than that sucky
> prime minister
>
> *tereshoppu / suka sōri yori / netsui ari*

By Akumu no Suka Seiken (Nightmarish Sucky Administration; "Minna de Seiji Senryū," no. 1079, January 2021). The reference here is to a famous TV announcer on Japanet Takata (Japan Netto Takata), the major Japanese teleshopping network, whose idiosyncratic zeal selling products, according to this verse, outstrips the zeal of the Suga administration in tackling the pandemic.

Teleworking and Telepartying

As might be expected, innumerable *sarasen* take up the issue of everyday life in Japan during the worldwide Covid-19 pandemic, minus the bile directed at leaders. One of the great themes has been telework (*terewāku*) or remote work (*rīmoto*), which while already on the rise, rose precipitously during the crisis. According to the annual survey conducted by Japan's Ministry of Land, Infrastructure, Transport and Tourism (Kokudo Kōtsūshō) cited in the Dai-Ichi Life press release, the percentage of all workers in Japan who telework jumped from around 15% in 2019 to over 22%

in 2020. Although the number had been surging from 14.2% in 2016 to 17.4% in 2018, it dipped to 15.4% in 2019. The sudden increase to 22.5% and reversal of the slight dip in 2019 no doubt can be attributed to the covid-19 pandemic.

On the one hand, working remotely from home puts the company in a less desirable light:

> working remotely,
> it's no longer essential:
> the workplace
>
> *rimōto de / fuyō fukyū ni / naru shokuba*

By Shū, who placed 85th in the 2020 contest.

On the other hand, the company may sometimes come out smelling like roses:

> teleworking
> one realizes the virtues
> of company chairs
>
> *terewāku / kizuita kaisha no / isu no yosa*

By Kubikata Korizō, "Stiff-Shoulder Dude" — a play on someone who suffers from stiff shoulders, suggesting someone who could benefit from a comfortable work chair. This verse placed 71st in the 2020 contest.

All this teleworking can, of course, be disorienting:

> what day is it?
> when working from home
> no clear answer
>
> *nanyōbi? / zaitaku kinmu de / wakaranaku*

SEVEN

This verse, by Kodaira Shukei Shokō (Officer Kodaira the Accountant), placed 74th in the 2020 contest.

Sometimes, the father of the house must apparently endure shenanigans right under his very nose, as per this verse, by Kitsume no Yaeba (Hard-assed Double-tooth):

> day off from work . . .
> my son with *Demon Slayer*
> my wife, *A Bit Tight*
>
> *kyūjitsu wa / musuko kimitsu de / yome kitsume*

The humor of this verse, which placed 25th in the 2020 contest, is that when the man of the house spends a day off from work at home, he realizes that while his son is engrossed in the vastly popular *Demon Slayer* (discussed next), in the form of either a comic book (*manga*) or animated series (*anime*), presumably instead of attending school or working—his wife is lost in the *Kimitsu* (A Bit Tight), which, as the title intimates, is an *eromanga* with S/M overtones.

Other verses mention *Demon Slayer* in domestic contexts, too, as with this one by Nekonosuke (Catboy) that placed 30th in the 2020 contest:

> family time:
> for the kid, *Demon Slayer*
> the couple, *Fissure*
>
> *ko wa kimetsu / fūfu wa kiretsu / ouchi jikan*

Beyond what the titles suggest about the interests of—and relationships among—members of this family, knowledge of both titles adds greater depth and hence appreciation. *Demon Slayer* (*Kimetsu no yaiba*), written and drawn by Gotōge Koyoharu (b.

1989), is a phenomenally popular *manga* for junior and senior high-school boys, serialized from 2016-2020 in the bestselling *manga* magazine *Weekly Shōnen Jump*. *Demon Slayer* is also an animated series, the first season running in Japan from April to September in 2019. The hero of the story, Kamado Tanjirō, is an orphan who decides to become a demon slayer. Conversely, *Fissure* (*Kiretsu*), written and drawn by Sakurai Mariko in 2014 and targeted to a female readership, is about a childless lesbian couple (at least initially: they eventually somehow get pregnant). Hence, the deeper pleasure of the verse has to do with exposing the dark secret desires of the child to be parentless and of the parents to be childless.

With the pandemic, the great theme of feeling alone in a crowd finds new ground at home:

> once upon a time
> when at home the family
> was all together . . .

hisabisa ni / kazoku ga sorotta / zaitaku de

Whereas in the before times the family was never together because they were never all at home at the same time, during the pandemic, the family was never together even though they were always at home at the same time. The verse, by Mō Hyaku Pāsento Shussha Oyaji (Already 100% Workbound Oldman), placed 75th in the 2020 contest.

The stay-at-home subsistence during the pandemic also throws new light onto the old theme of strained relations between a wife and her husband's mother:

SEVEN

> even at home
> chats with her daughter-in-law
> through a screen
>
> *jitaku demo / yome to no kaiwa / gamengōshi*

This verse, by Hottorain (Hotline), came in at 95th in the 2020 contest. Of course, *yome* can also refer to "bride," in which case the second line would read "chats with his new wife."

And speaking about digital screens (*gamen*), there's this bittersweet verse, which placed 42nd in the 2020 contest, by Deredere Jīchan (Doting Grampa):

> first time seeing
> my grandchild's face:
> on a smartphone
>
> *mago no kao / hajimete miru no wa / sumaho kōshi*

Without the "doting" in the penname, the verse might not attain such emotional depth.

And this one, a bit more sardonically:

> wonder when
> we can see faces unfiltered
> in real time?
>
> *itsu darō / dôki no sugao / mireru no wa*

This verse, by Nanchatte Daigaku Insei (Ersatz Grad Student), was 76th in the 2020 contest.

> working remotely,
> the ubiquitous background:
> highrise apartments

> *rimōto no / haikei dake wa / tawaman fū*

This verse, by Onkō, came in 88th in the 2020 contest. This unusual penname plays on the meaning of "mild mannered," substituting the Chinese graph for "dense" with "surge."

If a silver lining is to be found in working remotely, it is that one has a readymade excuse to avoid listening to certain things:

> one handy phrase
> for working remotely:
> "can't hear a thing!"

> *rimōto de / benrina kotoba / "kikoemasen!"*

This verse, by the appropriately named Rimōto no Tatsujin (Remote Master), apparently a man in his 50s, placed third in the 2020 competition.

Of course, not everyone who works remotely elects to keep the video feed on:

> You asleep?
> no response during
> the web meeting

> *neteiru no? / henji ga nai yo / Web kaigi*

Good thing that Rāno, the author of the verse (which placed 100th in the 2020 contest), used a pseudonym, lest the boss find out . . .

One can overstay one's welcome, even at home, as attested to by this verse — the grand prize winner of the 34th Dai-ichi Life *sarasen* contest — which speaks to the limbo in which so many workers in Japan suddenly found themselves:

> back to the office:
> the boss says *stay away!*
> the wife, *go on in!*

> *kaisha e wa / kuruna to jōshi / ike to tsuma*

In the aforementioned press release announcing the winning verses, Dai-ichi Life also included some demographic information about the contestants and voters, alike. This winning verse, by one Nakaji (short, perhaps, for Nakajima?), a poet in his 30s, placed first among readers in their 40s, 50s, and 60s, but not in their 20s or 30s. The earlier verse (two verses above), about deploying the excuse "can't hear a thing!" to avoid unpleasant conversations that was third overall, was also third among this younger crowd. The fact that both verses struck a chord with those in different age groups than the poets themselves suggests that, as might be expected, winning *sarasen* have an appeal beyond one's own immediate cohort.

A similar verse hardly minces words:

> "when the hell
> you goin' back to work?"
> pressure from the wife

> *shusshabi wa / tsugi wa itsu nano / tsuma no atsu*

This verse, by the aptly named Zaitaku Wākuman (Stay-at-home Workman), placed an honorable 21st in the 2020 contest. One would indeed be wise to yield to pressure from one's spouse:

> my cash payment
> without catching sight of it
> became my wife's!
>
> *jūman en / miru koto mo naku / tsuma no mono*

This verse, by Hakanaki Yume (Fleeting Dream), was the first runner-up — meaning it placed second — in the 2020 contest. The "cash payment" here refers to the Special Fixed Benefits (Tokubetsu Teigaku Kyūfukin) program — somewhat analogous to the "CARES" (Coronavirus Aid, Relief, and Economic Security) Act in the US — that paid ¥100,000 (about US $950) to each individual in Japan, regardless of employment status, age, gender, income, or number of members in a household.

> teleworking:
> the overgrown kids
> increase by one
>
> *terewāku / ōkina kodomo ga / hitori fue*

This verse, by Mītotekku (Meet Tech), placed 48th in the 2020 contest. Apparently, the bigger kids effectively have a new member among their ranks now that their father is no longer commuting to work.

> *hey sonny,*
> *c'mon, let's play!*
> the father at work
>
> *asobō yo / musuko yo, papa wa / shigotochū*

In the before times, most Japanese men would never be caught dead at home during the workday not to work. This verse, 80th in the 2020 contest, was written by one Poporun — a penname perhaps playing on Poporon-chan, a character in *Jashin-chan Doroppukikku* (Dropkick on My Devil!), a popular *manga* and *anime* series.

Some *sarasen* on the theme of families at home during the pandemic can be, well, touching:

> hard work
> becomes a labor of love —
> my kid's smiling face
>
> *hataraku ga / hataraku ni naru / ko no egao*

The author of this verse, which placed 26th in the 2020 contest, calls himself Sararimaru. While superficially sounding like the comic name of a stoic samurai as a kind of pun on *sarariman* (the clipped form of *sararīman*), Sararimaru can also be read as "easy" (*sarari*) "money" (*maru*) — making the poet's sudden realization that there is more to life than work all the more poignant. This is clearly another case in which the penname enriches the meaning of the verse.

One takeaway from the case of this verse by Sararimaru — and many of the other verses herein, as we have been seeing — is that the penname has effectively become another method of moving beyond the limitations of the short verseform, beyond the use of season words, a cut, and humor. Simply put, a penname specifically tailored to accompany a particular *sarasen* can be used to change the meaning of a verse, as well as to enhance its general ambiance.

> proclaiming
> "I love Nightplay!"
> his father panics
>
> *YOASOBI ga / daisuki to ii / chichi aseru*

The humor of this verse (by one Tenbi), which made the top ten finalists in the 2020 contest, placing 8th, here revolves around the father's literal interpretation of the capitalized term as "nighttime partying." Yet when written in this particular way, the term is actually the name of the pop duo YOASOBI ("Nightplay"), consisting of Vocaloid producer Ayase and singer-songwriter Ikura. Vocaloid, it should be mentioned, is a worldwide crowd-sourced collaborative songwriting software, producing massively popular J-pop songs sung by holographic pop stars, such as Hatsune Mitsu, who opened for Lady Gaga during one of that pop star's American tours.

The allusion to a J-pop group calls to mind the winner of the 32nd *sarasen* contest:

>after five already!
>*C'MON, BABY!*
>the latest distraction

>*goji sugita / kamonbeibī / USA barashi*

The particular challenge of understanding this seemingly meaningless verse (not to mention of rendering it into English) depends on knowledge of a hit J-pop song, by the group DA PUMP, titled "U.S.A."[28] Although "U.S.A." of course refers to the country, when read as Japanese, *usa* is the first part of the word *usabarashi*, meaning "to be entertained" or "to be distracted" (from one's worries). The song title itself deploys a gloss normally reserved for reading Chinese characters, though here is used to read the English letters. The *sarasen* was composed by a woman in her 60s calling herself Bon Odori (O-bon Dance), after the traditional dance, self-mockingly suggesting she's too old, or unskilled — or both? — to dance the popular dance that accompanies the "U.S.A." song.

---

28. For a music video of this song, visit: https://www.youtube.com/watch?v=sr--GVIoluU.

There are a couple of points of interest here. First, the fact that Bon Odori was in her sixties suggests the popularity of Japanese pop songs among the older generations as well as the ability of *sarasen* to span generations. Second, as I have been claiming, her penname seems to be individually tailored to this verse. Because *sarasen* tend to be one-offs, a poet can tailor her or his penname to provide information essential to the reading of the verse. This represents a break from early modern *senryū*, in which heteronyms typically poked fun at the poet but almost never provided pivotal information for the interpretation of any particular verse (beyond, say, the gender of the poet). Simply put, the *sarasen* has come to exploit the penname, long operative in early modern *senryū* and haiku, as an additional resource to overcome the brevity of 17 syllabets.

The pandemic has not only increased teleworking, it has perhaps occasioned the phenomenon of what might be dubbed "telepartying":

> Zoom drinking:
> one barhops merely by changing
> virtual backgrounds
>
> *zūmu nomi / haikei kaete / hashigozake*

This verse by Gōjikara Otoko (A Man From 5 p.m.), 91st in the 2020 contest, observes that drinking parties are such an important social and business activity, the custom carries on even during the age of teleconferencing.

Of course, just as one must not miss the last train home after a night of real partying, one must not miss the equivalent after a night of telepartying:

> last train home
> for an online drinking party:
> low batteries
>
> *shūden ga . . . / web nomikai dewa / jūden ga . . .*

By Chokkō Chokki (Non-stop Directly Home). This verse was tied for 97th place in the 2020 contest with the following verse:

> with no last train
> there's no end in sight:
> Zoom drinking party
>
> *owarenai / shūden ga nai / zūmu nomi*

By one Hige Daruma, "Bearded Bodhidharma," a heteronym that calls to mind the popular "Bodhidharma" tumbling doll that, like "Weebles," wobble but don't fall down. The implication, in the context of this verse, being a fall-down drunk who somehow never quite falls down.

Ultimately, even virtual drinking parties can get out of hand. At least according to the following verse, which placed 87th in the 2020 contest, by one Aketan (a slang term congratulating someone on the night before his or her birthday):

> the hell was that
> streaking across half naked?!
> online drinking party
>
> *ima no nani? / hanra yokogiru / Web nomikai*

Here, the word "Web," written in English letters, intrudes upon the Japanese, as though to reinforce the outlandishness of the abrupt nudity. Then again, since the Japanese word for web (*webu*) counts as two syllabets, using the one-syllable English word helps the verse avoid hypermeter (*jiamari*), meaning running over 17-syllabets. The flip side of outrageous online partying is unbearable solitude:

> venue searching
> for a night on the town
> at home

nomikai no / kaijō sagashi /ie no naka

A verse by Hidachi that placed 67th in the 2020 contest.

> I'll be back later
> and with a slide of the door
> telework!

"itte kuru" / fusuma ichimai / terewa-ku

This verse, by Kyōmo Shutsudō (Today Too Working Away From Home), which placed 34th in the 2020 contest, suggests that all one needs to do to commute to work during the pandemic is shut the sliding paper door (*fusuma*) between rooms.

As with early modern *senryū*, some *sarasen* point to the grass always being greener, or the pleasures of giving in to reverse psychology, or inevitably longing for what one does not have, as with the following specimen (68th in the 2020 contest), by Naimono Nedari (Longing For What One Has Not):

> once you realize
> there's no need to commute
> you kinda want to!

tsūkin mo / shinakute ii to /shitaku naru

In all my time living and working in Japan (admittedly in the before times), I never once heard anyone profess a love for the daily commute.

Then again, brand new employees fresh out of college, who typically start working for companies in April, might not have had the chance to commute long enough to get tired of it before the pandemic hit that very month:

> a working adult
> having gone into work
> only five times!

> *shakaijin / shussha shita no wa / mada gokai*

By Tere Shin'nyū Shain (Telecommuting New Employee), a heteronym that provides necessary context for understanding the verse (86th in the 2020 contest).

The mishaps of working from home are legion:

> rough draft —
> the send button hit
> by the cat

> *shitagaki no / sōshinkī o / neko ga oshi*

By Yudan Zaitaku (At-home Klutz), this verse placed 19th in the 2020 contest.

> working remotely
> forgetting to hit the mute button
> complaints outed

> *rimōto de / myūto wasurete / buchi bareru*

SEVEN

This verse (46th in the 2020 contest) is by one Nebo — perhaps a lazy form of *neboke* (sleepyhead).

Unmasking the Naked Truth

Another common theme connected to life during the pandemic is the use of facial masks. The Japanese, like the Chinese, South Koreans, Taiwanese, and other East Asian neighbors, it should be pointed out, have long used facial masks out of consideration for those around them, even in the before times. Since the pandemic began, the necessity for masks has of course only increased, as attested to by this verse, 58th in the 2020 contest, by Moyashi (Beansprout):

> at each restaurant
> the same dress code:
> a mask
>
> *dono mise mo / doresukōdo wa / masuku ari*

Increased mask usage has occasioned an outpouring of verses on that theme:

> being told
> *You're so young*
> the mask stays on!
>
> *owakai to / iware masuku o / hazusenai*

Written by one Echiketto (Etiquette), a heteronym that humorously suggests mask wearing is a matter of good manners and certainly not, say, a matter of vanity. This verse placed 9th overall in the 2020 contest.

Here's another good-natured self-mocking mask verse, which placed a respectable 22nd in the 2020 contest:

> it's the mask,
> they say, that makes my face
> so damn handsome!
>
> *masuku da to / yoku iwaremasu / ikemen ne*

The punchline of this verse, *ikemen* (written in the original verse in *katakana*), means "good-looking guy," but also puns on "face" (*omote*), one possible Chinese character for *men*. Unsurprisingly, the author of the verse calls himself Sonoman (That Guy).

On the other hand, some folks may beg to differ with such haughty self-appraisal, as with this gem by Waisan. (Since *wai* is rendered in *katakana*, it has a range of meanings, from "I," to "Why?" and even "Y"):

> wearing a mask
> is hardly protection enough—
> a wife's grumble
>
> *masuku de wa / fusegi kirenai / tsuma no guchi*

This was 38th in the 2020 contest.

> ear aches . . .
> relentless mask wearing
> and wife's grumbling
>
> *mimi itai / jōji masuku to / tsuma no guchi*

This verse, by Samī, placed 41st in the 2020 contest.

SEVEN

> donning a mask
> the expression of my boss
> can't be discerned

> *masuku shite / jōshi no kaoiro / yomitorezu*

This verse, 64th in the 2020 contest, was written by one Yareba Dekiru (If You Try You Can Do It). This phrase recalls one of Prime Minister Suga's inane lines during the second Covid wave in Japan (in July 2020), in which he infamously said of the ill-fated Go-To travel campaign: "If you try, you can do it, right?" (*yareba dekiru janai ka*). (Something analogous in American political history might be Nancy Reagan's infamous "Just say no" campaign against drugs.) As mentioned above, this line became the title of Suga's book, *Where There's a Will There's a Way*.

> on smartphones
> failing to authenticate me:
> my own wife!

> *sumaho yori / ore o ninshō / shinai tsuma*

This verse, 73rd in the 2020 contest, was by Yamamune Unsui (Yamamune the Wandering Monk) — a name implying something like the Flying Dutchman, who was trapped in the limbo of perpetual nationless exile.

Masaru Kuwesto (Masaru Quest) observes something profound about the difference between privacy and paranoia, between intimacy and overprotection:

> only their masks
> do wife and daughter
> wash separately

> *masuku sae / tsuma to musume to / betsuarai*

This verse was 61st in the 2020 contest.

Fears of viral transmission even plague married couples, masked or not:

> my wife
> who used to fistbump me
> now keeps her distance
>
> *gūtacchi / tsuma wa watashi ni / nōtacchi*

The fun of this verse, by Isshō Disutansu (Lifelong Distancing), 23rd in the 2020 contest, has to do with the extreme contrast in meaning between the similar sounding words *gūtacchi*, "fistbump," and *nōtacchi*, "no touch."

And another verse on separation within the same household:

> calling for you
> with no reason in particular —
> social distancing
>
> *anata to wa / yōsei nakutemo / disutansu*

This verse, by Otō (Papa), placed 43rd in the 2020 contest.

> my father —
> his mask and conversations
> both slightly off
>
> *otōsan / masuku mo kaiwa mo / yoku zureru*

This verse, by Sagojō, placed 7th overall in the 2020 contest. Incidentally, Sagojō, the name of a character in the great sixteenth-century Chinese novel Journey to the West (*Xi You Ji*; known in Japan as *Saiyūki*), is more recently the name of the King of

SEVEN

Kappa (water sprite) monsters (Kapaō Sagojō) in *Yokai Watch*, a tremendously popular nexus of role playing video games, action figurines, and so on.

Here's a verse that would not have made much sense in the before times, but requires little explanation in the age of coronavirus:

> coughing fit —
> it's the dirty looks that hurt
> aboard a train
>
> *sekikonde / shisen ga itai / denshanai*

This verse, by Aiinshū Tain (Thirsty Booze-loving Guzzler), placed 40th in the 2020 contest.

> feverishness
> in the before times meant work
> now, quarantine
>
> *netsuppoi / mukashi wa kaisha / ima taiki*

This verse, 62nd in the 2020 contest, is by one Metabo (Metabolic Syndrome), a euphemism for someone overweight.

The pandemic has changed the relationship between work life and homelife, of course, but here's a verse that focuses on the changing overlap between the two:

> once upon a time
> "take home orders" referred to work
> but now to meals
>
> *mochikaeri / mukashi wa shigoto / ima wa meshi*

By Shufu to Shufu (House Hubbie and House Wife), this verse came in 66th in the 2020 contest. It used to be work that many employees in hardworking Japan brought back home with them where they would eat. But during the pandemic, it's the food that most people now bring home in order to work. The topsy-turviness comes across better in Japanese because most folks in English-speaking countries tend to bring home more food than work. But the real "kicker" in the original verse is that the term *meshi*, a masculine term for "cooked rice" and, by extension, for meals or food in general, can also mean "livelihood," or living. Hence, the phrase "take-home orders" in the before times referred to one's bread and butter, whereas now it refers to, well, one's bread and butter.

Similarly, Megane Kazoku (Glasses Family) protests:

> *Go fetch!*
> What am I, the family
> Uber driver?!
>
> *katte kite / ore wa waga ie no / ūbā ka*

This verse placed 31st in the 2020 contest.

For those concerned about dining out during the pandemic, the only alternative to take home is home delivery, a practice undoubtedly more widespread among the younger generations:

> doorstep delivery
> taken for something suspicious—
> hysterical granny!
>
> *okihai o / fushinbutsu da to / sawagu baba*

The heteronym here, Ūbabaītsu, "Granny Uber Eats," amounts to more self-mocking humor, since it puns on Ūbāītsu, the food delivery service Uber Eats (which operates in Japan as well as many other countries), replacing the *bā* of Ūbā (i.e. the ber of Uber) with *baba* (grandma). Here, again, the penname provides essential information to understanding the verse, which placed 65th in the 2020 contest.

Whereas Granny Uber Eats is distressed by the mysterious package on her doorstep, it is such things as large corporations — and a certain foreign president — that arouse alarm (presumably not just among the geriatric) in the following verse:

> what's terrifying:
> Google, Amazon,
> Xi Jinping

> *kowai no wa / gūguru amazon / Shū Kinpei*

By one Kiyo ("Minnaj de Seiji Senryū," no. 1052, December 2020).

Five Ring *Sarasen* (*Gorin Sarasen*)

Sarasen on the various problems associated with the ill-fated 2020 Tokyo Olympics are legion. The Marusen site alone lists over 500 verses under the keyword Olympics (*orinpikku*). In fact, given that part of the 2020 games are slated to take place in Miyagi Prefecture, the official prefectural website has provided space for such *sarasen*, as with the following two verses, expressing dissatisfaction both with the unavailability and cost of tickets and with the insistence that the show must go on in spite of the government's mishandling of the pandemic response:

> tickets
> completely sold out
> I'll buy a TV

> *chiketto wa / hazurete shimai / terebi kau*

By Reoparuto Kazuko Mama-san (Leopard Kazuko's Mom) from Sendai City, Izumi district. The implication being that one must watch the games on TV because the tickets, which could only be won through a lottery, were more expensive than a TV set in the first place. The verse, it should be mentioned, was written before the pandemic made staying at home more desirable than attending.

> just standing there
> you're already
> a medalist
>
> *soko ni tatsu / anata wa mō / medarisuto*

This verse, by an unnamed male from Sendai City, Wakabayashi District, suggests that attending the Olympics in the age of Covid is itself worthy of a medal.

> Covid negative —
> more valuable than
> a gold medal!
>
> *korona insei / kin medaru yori / kachi ga aru*

By Burendo Monaka (Blend-coffee Wafer-cake), a heteronym that suggests someone lazing about , perhaps, rather than bending over backwards to attend the games. ("Marusen" March 2021).

> more than life:
> the Go-To campaign and games
> the top priority
>
> *inochi yori / Go-To gorin ga / saiyūsen*

SEVEN

By Takane no Bara (High-peak Rosebush — playing off the phrase *takane no hana*, a beautiful woman who is out of reach of most men. Her relationship, if any, to the early modern *senryū* poet Takane from Sakurada, mentioned in Yanagidaru 12, is unclear). This verse unearths a similarity of sounds in two misbegotten national projects: the "five rings" (*gorin*), meaning the Olympics (specifically the 2020 Tokyo games, delayed until summer 2021); and the "Go-To Travel" campaign.[29] The Japanese government launched the campaign in July of 2020 to try to stimulate domestic tourism as a means of compensating for the economically devastating decline in international tourism during the pandemic. The campaign essentially paid half of all travel costs (35% off the total cost plus 15% in additional coupons) to all residents of Japan. The campaign was suspended shortly before the present *sarasen* ("Minna de Seiji Senryū," no. 1069) was published on January 5, 2021.

> corona deaths —
> it's our higher cultural level
> that keeps 'em so low

> *korona shisha / sukunai no wa / "mindō ga chigau kara"*

By Sensunai Kapone (No-sense Capone). The reference here ("Minna de Seiji Senryū," no. 1027, June 2020) is to a controversial statement (*mondai hatsugen*) by Deputy Prime Minister (and Finance Minister) Asō Tarō that made headlines in June 2020 for its cultural arrogance. Asō attributed Japan's low Covid-19 death rate with respect other countries to Japan's "superior level of culture" (*mindō*). Ironically, it may well be the sociopolitical satire of *sarasen* — like this very verse poking fun at Japanese governmental leaders — that imbues Japan with some of its cultural depth in the first place.

---

29. http://www.fujii-hiroki.net/senryuuBBS/epad.cgi.

Conclusion

What has our preliminary exploration of *sarasen* in comparison to early modern *senryū* demonstrated? To return to my three overarching points, first, the use of pennames has been an enduring feature of *senryū* from its inception in the eighteenth century through the present day. Contrary to the conventional wisdom about haiku, with its bias against the *senryū* in English-language scholarship as doggerel by anonymous wags, the *senryū* was not only the first mass-produced and mass-consumed form of standalone playful linked verse, but was most decidedly not anonymous. The majority of verses in *Yanagidaru*—the main repository of early modern *senryū*—had clear pennames. I would argue that even those that did not, however, must have been submitted to versecapping judges with a penname. Moreover, some verses that appear to have been published without a penname in *Yanagidaru* are published in the same or another collection *with* a penname.

Admittedly, my focus on *Yanagidaru* does not provide a complete picture of early modern pennames. Ideally, a full reckoning of pennames in all *senryū* collections over and beyond *Yanagidaru* would allow us more nuanced conclusions. Until then, however, my preliminary conclusion that most *senryū*, far from being anonymous (as the conventional wisdom has had it), are in fact named, at least in the form of pennames. Although early modern *senryū* pennames tend to have functioned primarily as heteronyms and brand names, since as pseudonyms they were relatively ineffectual, modern *sarasen* pennames tend to be heteronyms, more than brand names, tailored to augment the meaning of individual verses. To what extent these *sarasen* function as pseudonyms, however, remains unclear. For instance, in the case of at least one verse — the one about falling asleep during web meetings — we can imagine that the penname functions effectively as a pseudonym, protecting the author Rāno from unpleasant consequences from his boss at work. Interestingly, then, the pseudonym may have acquired a more important function in some contemporary *sarasen*, since the threat is no longer an authoritarian government doling out capital punishment.

Hence, based on my discussion of *sarasen* pennames translated herein, we can conclude that while, contrary to the prevailing wisdom, pennames have been an enduring feature of *senryū* from their inception and massive popularity during the eighteenth century to the present day, what has changed is the tendency toward tailoring pennames to supplement or even clarify the meaning of a *sarasen*. In the hands of shrewd *sarasen* authors, the penname is increasingly becoming another resource for overcoming the brevity of the 17-syllabet verseform. It may be only a matter of time before the same becomes true of haiku, perhaps, although commercial and other pressures to associate a corpus of literary works with a single brand name — be it a penname or a poet's actual name — seems to remain a countervailing force to be reckoned with.

Second, we have seen a progression in *senryū* and *sarasen* from indirect to direct satire. Classic *senryū* composed in the eighteenth and nineteenth centuries did not name names, as it were, whereas *sarasen* in the twentieth and twenty-first centuries increasingly do so. It is tempting to conclude that the micro-usage of pennames, meaning individuated pennames tailored to particular verses, has allowed the *sarasen* to be more direct in its satire. However, this must be contextualized in broader terms of the transition in Japanese governance from authoritarian feudal regime to modern constitutionally based democratic monarchy. This is not to say that all *sarasen* authors always tailor their pennames to each and every individual verse. In the verses translated herein, we have seen multiple verses, by the poets Takane no Bara (High-peak Rosebush) and Akumu no Suka Seiken (Nightmarish Sucky Administration), for instance, published under the same penname. Still, the majority of *sarasen* pennames seem to be one-offs.

What is astounding, perhaps—and this is my third and final point—is that the *sarasen* has seemed to emerge not only as a major mode of mainstream sociopolitical criticism in Japan, but perhaps as the major mode, eclipsing even the form of political satire in the newspaper editorial cartoon. The *senryū* generally speaking, in both its classic and salaryman forms, has been an enduring form of sociopolitical satire that should be taken at least as seriously as mainstream political cartoons when it comes to understanding the average person's thinking about society and politics.

It may even be the case that *sarasen* and classic *senryū* reside closer to the heart of playful linked verse (*haikai*) than the verse mode now known as haiku. In fact, one way of reading the classic Zen nature haiku is as an apolitical mode that applies the *senryū* spirit of the exposé to other matters. If you want to learn about the pine, go to the pine; if you want to learn about hypocrisy, go to the hypocrites. Hence, if a binary must be constructed, rather than defining haiku as being about Nature and *senryū* about human nature, it may be more accurate to define *senryū* as being about hypocrisy, contradictions, and paradoxes and haiku about the same topics as seen by their absence. Both haiku and *senryū* ultimately comment on universal truths, and playfully so, though their material differs.

The modern *sarasen* is interested in unearthing hypocrisy, as well. Yet like the early modern *senryū*, it also is sensitive to heartache. *Sarasen* may help one gain a sense of literary control over life's uncontrollable absurdities, even things like 3-11, the Covid-19 pandemic, the ongoing disappointments with the 2020 Tokyo Olympics, and other such catastrophes. To many readers, it may seem that writing comic haiku on national traumas is disrespectful to the victims and their survivors, just as the major Japanese newspapers maintain. Yet setting aside the phenomenon of black humor, which is one way that some people deal with life's tragedies, there is the observation that laughter helps cover up the existential aloneness (*sabi*) that animates so many of the best haiku. In this respect, the *senryū* and haiku are most profoundly not dissimilar. This observation was known in early modern Japan, too, as attested to by the following *senryū* by one Chigusa, who shall have the final say:

> laughing loudly
> that the loneliness
> might be forgotten
>
> *takawarai / shite sabishisa o / wasureru ki*

Works Cited

The place of publications for all Japanese-language works is Tokyo unless otherwise stated.

Addiss, The *Art of Haiku: Its History Through Poems and Paintings by Japanese Masters*. Shambala, 2012.

Blyth, R.H. *Oriental Humour*. Hokuseido Press, 1959.

_____. *Senryu: Japanese Satirical Verses*. Hokuseido, 1949.

Duus, Peter. "Presidential Address: Weapons of the Weak, Weapons of the Strong: The Development of the Japanese Political Cartoon. *The Journal of Asian Studies* (2001), vol. 60, no. 4, pp. 965-997.

Farge, William J. *A Christian Samurai: The Trials of Baba Bunkō*. Washington, D.C.: The Catholic University of America Press, 2016.

Galbraith, Patrick W. and Jason G. Karlin, ed., *Media Convergence in Japan*. Kinema Club, 2016.

Gardner, Richard A. "The Blessing of Living in a Country Where There Are Senryū: Humor in the Response to Aum Shinrikyō," in *Asian Folklore Studies* (April 2002), pp. 35-75.

Gilbert, Richard. "Stalking the Wild Onji: The Search for Current Linguistic Terms Used in Japanese Poetry Circles." In *Frogpond: Journal of the Haiku Society of America*, vol. 22: Supplement (1999), pp. 7-32.

Hamada Giichirō. "Senryū no dokkai—nazoku no kaishaku ni tsuite." In *Edo bungeikō: Kyōka, senryū, gesaku* (Iwanami shoten, 1988), pp. 125-144.

Hamada Giichirō, Suzuki Katsutada and Mizuno Minoru, eds., *Nihon koten bungaku zenshū 46, Kibyōshi senryū kyōka*. Shōgakukan, 1971.

Keene, Donald. *World Within Walls: Japanese Literature of the Pre-Modern Era, 1600-1867*. Tokyo: Charles E. Tuttle, 1978 (first published by Holt, Reinhart and Winston, 1976), pp. 525-534.

Kern, Adam L. *The Penguin Book of Haiku*. London: Penguin Classics, 2018.

Okada Hajime, ed. *Haifū yanagidaru zenshū*. Sanseidō, 1976-1984. 13 volumes.

Ramirez-Christensen, Esperanza. *Emptiness and Temporality: Buddhism and Medieval Japanese Poetry*. Palo Alto: Stanford University Press, 2008.

Shimizu Isao. *Manga no rekishi. In Iwanami shinsho 172*. Iwanami shoten, 1991.

Shirane, Haruo, ed., *Early Modern Japanese Literature: An Anthology*. New York: Columbia University, 2002.

Stewart, Ronald. "Post 3-11 Japanese Political Cartooning with Satiric Bite: Non-Newspaper Cartoons and Their Potential." In *Kritika Kultura* 26 (2016), pp. 179-220.

Ueda, Makoto. *Light Verse from the Floating World: An Anthology of Premodern Japanese Senryu*. New York: Columbia University Press, 1999.

Wattles, Miriam. *The Life and Afterlives of Hanabusa Itchō, Artist-Rebel of Edo*. Leiden: Brill, 2013.

Yamaguchi, Mari. "Japan virus outbreaks, scandals sap public support for Suga," December 29, 2020, Associated Press.

Yamamoto Seinosuke. *Senryū meiji sesōshi*. Makino shuppan, 1983.

Yamashita Kazumi, *Bashō hyaku meigen*. Fujimi Shobō, 1996.

I'd like to thank the two anonymous readers as well as my spouse, Tomoko Wakana Kern, for their helpful suggestions.

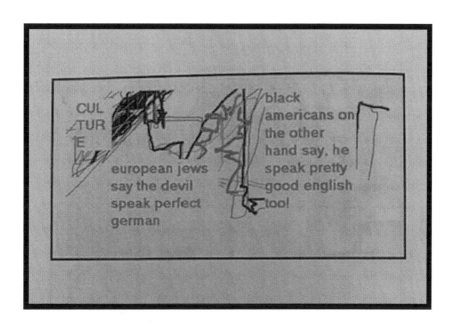

Poet/Artist: Amiri Baraka

LIVING IN COMMUNITY:

The More-than-Human World in Gerald Vizenor's Haiku

AMANDA MONTELEONE

ABSTRACT: Gerald Vizenor's haiku, first published in the 1960s, question a human-centered perspective by reimagining ordinary sights from the perspectives of other-than-human creatures. Vizenor, of Anishinaabe descent, is an influential writer, scholar, and activist whose work pertains to Indigenous affairs in North America. While scholars have analyzed Vizenor's haiku through the lens of Native American literature and theory, often observing how Vizenor's haiku engages with concepts found in his other work, such as survivance or the "vanishing Indian," an ecocritical perspective on Vizenor's haiku clarifies how its presentation of the more-than-human world has some similarities to the Anishinaabe philosophy of mino-bimaadiziwin, or the Good Life. This essay examines how Vizenor's haiku communicates this perspective by focusing on small details relevant to other-than-human lives; by describing how other-than-human creatures utilize and share spaces with others, including humans; and by suggesting that artistic creations, sometimes mediated by humans, ultimately emerge from the more-than-human world. I argue that many of Vizenor's haiku pose the experiences of other-than-human beings as important sources of knowledge for living in community with others, thus sharing certain teachings of the Good Life. While Vizenor's haiku, like many of his other writings, contradict Western rational definitions of life and community, they also exemplify the development of one's knowledge about the more-than-human world through the close observation of ordinary sights in nature, offering a constructive perspective on the issue.

Living Within Community

> cocky wren
> inspects a tiny bird house
> scent of pine (*Favor* 5)

Gerald Vizenor's haiku, first published in the 1960s, question a human-centered perspective by reimagining ordinary sights from the perspectives of other-than-human creatures. For instance, in the above poem, the first two lines describe an animal subject and the subject's action in a scene, while the third line suggests what the reader might notice about the scene from the wren's perspective. By this, the haiku indicates an interest not only in the wren's behavior but how one might experience the world from the wren's position. The poem is playful and inquisitive in its consideration of how other-than-human creatures experience the world around them, provoking questions that humans may never be able to answer but that are nonetheless important to ask to grow in understanding about the natural world and our place in it.

Gerald Vizenor's haiku incorporate qualities from the dream song, a part of the oral tradition of the Anishinaabe, a group of Indigenous people living in Canada and North America, and from the Japanese haiku tradition. Vizenor, of Anishinaabe descent, is an influential writer, scholar, and activist whose work pertains to Indigenous affairs in North America. This way of presenting connections between various living things in a more-than-human world in Vizenor's haiku is like the Anishinaabe philosophy of mino-bimaadiziwin, or the Good Life, which some Anishinaabe writers have described as a lifelong process of learning to live in community with humans, ancestors, and the other-than-human. Living the Good Life includes increasing one's ability to learn to live in a community from observing the other-than-human, an idea suggested by many of Vizenor's haiku.

Throughout the essay, I use the terms "more-than-human" and "other-than-human" as they are commonly used in ecocritical literary analyses — that is, to complicate and/or subvert the human/animal binary that features in Western logocentric thinking. These terms are derived from David Abram's philosophical works *The Spell of the Sensuous: Perception and Language in a More-than-Human World* and *Becoming Animal: An Earthly Cosmology*. *The Spell of the Sensuous* considers how Western cultures have an unnecessarily limited perspective of all life outside of human society. Our underused human senses, Abram finds, can draw more information from a larger, nonhuman world, the "more-than-human" world, than the Western rational viewpoint considers. In *Becoming Animal*, Abram advocates an awareness of ourselves as animals, subverting the Western consciousness of the "great chain of being," a hierarchy of life forms based on the degree of "spirit" these forms are believed to possess (46-47). Describing animals as "other-than-human" creatures provides a means to acknowledge both human animality and animal subjectivity from a perspective seeking to move beyond the traditional Western human/animal binary.

Vizenor's haiku, which incorporate elements from the Anishinaabe oral tradition as well as the Japanese tradition, are also oriented in a discourse of English-language haiku that began in the early twentieth century with Ezra Pound and other Imagist writers. Bruce Ross notes that ". . . Ezra Pound's manifesto on Imagism argued that poetry must address its subject forthrightly . . . in order to distance itself from nineteenth-century conventions of sentimentality and cliched figurative expression" (xvi). Joan Giroux, Kenneth Yasuda, and others have argued that Ezra Pound's well-known Imagist poem "In a Station of the Metro" does not constitute a haiku because the association between the imagery of the two lines is too loose. However, Pound's famous lines seem to constitute an important predecessor for Vizenor's own work, since Vizenor dedicates his most recent haiku book *Favor of Crows* to Ezra Pound as one of "Six

Poets and Teachers" and includes Pound's well-known poem as an epigraph. Vizenor seems less concerned with striving to be true to a Japanese model and more interested in what Vizenor describes as the "imagistic literary connections" he finds between Japanese haiku and Anishinaabe dream songs (*Favor* xi). The dream song in English prose has a connection to the history of English language haiku prior to Vizenor's work. Frances Densmore, an ethnomusicologist, recorded dream songs from the Ojibway people in the early twentieth century (Blaeser 110). Densmore's translations, emerging around the same time as the work of Imagist poets, have been described as haiku-like (Blaeser 111). Kimberly Blaeser suggests this potential source of inspiration when noting that "[t]he imagists, who were fascinated with the haiku as well as with other 'primitive' forms such as . . . Native American song poems, championed a new form of poetry . . ." (111). While not haiku in the strictest of terms, Imagist poetry serves as an English-language predecessor to Vizenor's own haiku both in radically transforming the nature of English-language poetry as well as turning to non-Western forms for inspiration.

Vizenor's haiku share characteristics with other English-language haiku in the latter half of the twentieth century such as the transcendence of normal perceptions of objects and increased specificity in describing nature. Summarizing the characteristics of several generations of English-language haiku poets that have succeeded the Imagist poets, Ross notes how American poets have attempted to distance themselves from Western poetic traditions of previous generations by striving toward the values of Japanese haiku. However, American haiku writers have not necessarily been aiming to craft haiku in a Japanese tradition. As a Native American poet writing in the English language, Vizenor shares some characteristics with American haiku poets, particularly with the generation that Ross notes emerging in the late fifties and early sixties, around the time Vizenor published his first haiku books. Ross describes this generation as evoking "cosmic revelations about external and internal reality . . . that . . . are expressed as a transcendence of the normal self and of the normal perception of objects" (xx). Like the work of these poets, Vizenor's haiku strive to transform the reader's perceptions of everyday natural surroundings. The "cosmic revelations" for which Vizenor strives are informed by Anishinaabe values of maintaining a proper relationship to the world. Allan Burns notes that increasing specificity within the nature tradition became important in English-language haiku in the late sixties and seventies (56). For instance, poets "wrote with field-guide precision of muskellunge and mourning cloaks" (Burns 57). Vizenor's haiku often assume this kind of precision; for instance, the maple beetle and downy woodpecker mentioned in poems in this essay are familiar North American animals. In Vizenor's haiku, specificity is less conspicuous than the examples Burns gives, seeming to tie more personal or regional associations to the haiku scene.

Another quality of the English-language haiku tradition Vizenor's work expresses is the haiku moment. Giroux notes how English-language haiku poets have struggled to reinterpret this element from Japanese haiku. Differences between the Japanese and English languages, as well as philosophical and aesthetic traditions unique to Japan, create certain challenges for English-language poets, Giroux finds, stating that "[t]he danger of conscious striving for paradox, intellection and explicit judgment in writing English haiku cannot be overemphasized" (54). English-language poets wishing to distance themselves from Western literary tradition should strive instead, Giroux argues, for directness without metacommentary, an idea closely united to Zen philosophy. Giroux links the Zen notion of *satori*, an experience of sudden comprehension or enlightenment, to the "haiku moment," an "instant in which man becomes united to an object, virtually becomes the object and realizes the eternal, universal truth contained in being" (45-46). Kimberly Blaeser has noted that Vizenor's poetry engages with the idea of enlightenment from Zen Buddhism to create a kind of haiku moment that informs the reader's perceptions about the world. Blaeser finds that the contrast of expectations and reality between the first two and final lines of Vizenor's haiku "have the effect of eliciting an internal gasp of recognition or an inadvertent glottal stop, either of which then provides the momentum for bridging the gap between mere words and experiential reality" (121). Vizenor's haiku, via these expressions of the haiku moment, communicate an ethic of living in respectful community with the other-than-human that reflects the values of the Good Life.

Vizenor's haiku communicate an ethic of learning to live in community with others by borrowing qualities from both Anishinaabe and Japanese cultural traditions. For instance, the qualities of humor and compassion expressed in Vizenor's haiku are similar to those expressed in the haiku of Japanese poets Matsuo Bashō (1644–1694), Yosa Buson (1716–1784) and Kobayashi Issa (1763–1828), writers Vizenor has described at length in his own haiku books. There is also a teasing, often tricky, quality to many of Vizenor's haiku like the trickster figure of Native American oral traditions. In the Anishinaabe oral tradition, the antics of the trickster figure, Nanabozho, reveal new perspectives on life and teach people not to take themselves too seriously. In expressing these qualities, Vizenor's haiku communicate an ethic of respect for and understanding of community in the natural world that contradicts Western logocentricity, a view that Vizenor, in other writings, has criticized as destructive. Many of Vizenor's haiku pose the perspectives of other-than-human beings as important sources of knowledge for living in community with others in a manner like certain teachings of the Good Life.

To demonstrate how Vizenor's haiku present an ethic of respect toward a larger community of the more-than-human, the essay first explores scholarship on mino-bimaadiziwin, the Anishinaabe philosophy of the Good Life, as well as ecocritical scholarship on Vizenor's other work and Vizenor's critique of Western logocentricity. Next, the essay considers Vizenor's responsiveness to Bashō, Buson, and Issa, three haiku poets Vizenor has often referenced in his own writings as influential in his own haiku endeavors. The comparison of Vizenor's poems to those of these poets clarifies how Vizenor's own take on observing nature or feeling compassion for the other-than-human dialogues with Edo period haiku that also closely observe nature or express compassion for nonhuman beings. Vizenor's poems articulate a concept similar to the teachings of the Good Life in emphasizing how the recognition of other-than-human perspectives and behaviors can inform our understanding of how to live in community with others, human and nonhuman.

Brent Debassige considers the importance of utilizing the principles of the Good Life in ethnographic research of Native people, while Marc Kruse, Nicholas Tanchuk, and Robert Hamilton argue for the Good Life as an essential teaching in Native education. According to these writers, mino-bimaadiziwin is a way of life that privileges the awareness of one's position within a community of humans and nonhumans. Wellness is measured not only by physical health but also by one's connections with a larger community. As an individual continues along a journey of mino-bimaadiziwin, the individual develops a deeper understanding of the other-than-human as kin and teachers. The realities of the other-than-human thus become an important source of knowledge for the individual seeking to live in community with others. Debassige, in presenting the Good Life as a research method toward the Anishinaabe people, first describes his own identity and orientation within larger communities. Debassige states that this is to acknowledge that he is "one voice that is part of many interrelated realities" and that his "origin of learning about a way of knowing" comes from an individual perspective (Debassige 12). Debassige describes mino-bimaadiziwin as a concept that "contains the past, present, and future of Good and respectful approaches in daily life" (16) and also as "a life-long educational journey" (18). Kruse et al. emphasize how mino-bimaadiziwin instructs that "the value of human lives is rightly determined by our respect for and protection of all living things, as in a kinship relationship" (588). In other words, a human's personal value increases in proportion to the human's rightful thoughts and actions toward all life, including the other-than-human. Kruse et al. state that "life is not given to us to individually possess; instead, we are called to give ourselves to our relationships with the diversity of life" (589). In other words, those who live the Good Life are expected to increase their knowledge of how their lives are interrelated with other lives and to strive to act with the responsibility this knowledge brings.

Before I continue further with the background on Vizenor's haiku, I want to acknowledge my own identity and individual perspective regarding this research topic, as Debassige advocates. As a white, middle-class, American woman with a Protestant upbringing, I do not have first-hand knowledge of Anishinaabe or other Indigenous cultures. My discussion of the Good Life and of Vizenor's writings is informed by the works of Indigenous and non-Indigenous scholars. My goal in writing this essay is to explicate how Vizenor's haiku orient reader perceptions of nature and communities in an ethic toward the environment. My interest in the portrayal of nature in Vizenor's haiku comes from my interest in earth-based philosophies and ethics toward the environment. The ecocritical lens is comfortable for me to assume because it is utilized in an academic setting and has connections with both the Western rational viewpoint and my personal beliefs. Those with first-hand knowledge of an Indigenous tradition may have a richer, more informed experience of a text inspired by an Anishinaabe oral tradition than myself. Due to my lack of context or biased worldview, my work may omit relevant information about the Good Life or connections between the Good Life and Vizenor's poems. Nevertheless, I believe my use of the ecocritical lens and available scholarship is a productive means to analyze Vizenor's nature-oriented haiku in a discourse of twentieth-century English-language haiku.

Unlike the philosophy of the Good Life, Western logocentricity does not consider a community with the other-than-human in its production of knowledge. Just as Kruse et al. point to the differences between the Good Life and the Western rational view as it originates with Plato, Vizenor's other work, such as *Bearheart: The Heirship Chronicles*, according to Dreese, portrays the damage to the environment and human and nonhuman communities that the Western rational viewpoint causes. In considering the differences between the Anishinaabe and Eurocentric models of knowledge production, Kruse et al. consider how, in Plato's analogy of the cave, the learner, freed from the darkness of the cave by rational thought, joins with other humans to build a good society, without connection to the other-than-human world. Kruse et al. note that "the image of turning away from the subjectivity of more-than-human life in order to ascend to an intellectual realm in which such lives are objectified and ethically mute is . . . a persistent theme in Western thought, education, and politics" (590). This idea, according to the authors, also supports the practices of Western colonialism, to the detriment of Indigenous human lives in North America as well as to the more-than-human world. Similarly, Vizenor's novel *Bearheart*, Dreese argues, portrays a journey of pilgrims through a post-apocalyptic world affected by Western technology, a product of Western logocentricity. Dreese notes Vizenor's use of the trickster figure in *Bearheart* in the form of the character Proude Cedarfair, who brings attention to the destructive nature of Western thinking and "represents American Indian views of nature based on reciprocity and respect, knowing that conquering nature is an illusion" (21). Interpreting *Bearheart* from an ecocritical viewpoint, Dreese observes that ecocritical concepts like "deep ecology" challenge Western logocentricity and the separation of humans from other aspects of nature in a manner similar to some Native American beliefs.

While ecocritical concepts like "deep ecology" are developed by Western academics and thus originate at least in part from a

SEVEN

Western logocentric institution, Dreese's analysis of Bearheart indicates Vizenor's interest in portraying the damage caused by Western colonialism to communities of humans and nonhumans as well as investigating more holistic alternatives. Vizenor's haiku, in privileging the perspectives of the other-than-human, similarly expresses this interest in finding ways for humans to live more sustainably by exposing how one's actions affect others in the more-than-human world. Kruse et al. clarify how the philosophy of the Good Life relates to the production of this kind of knowledge in stating that "[a]ll living things aim to track reality — all love to live by the truth — and, as we can tell by observing plants and animals, all respond to reality in ways meant to preserve their capacities to do so" (599). In other words, the Good Life produces knowledge to aid in one's survival in the more-than-human world, a subject of increasing urgency as human and nonhuman communities in the world feel the effects of ecological collapse. While *Bearheart* portrays a grim, postapocalyptic picture of how Western logocentricity, in the form of colonialism, brings about ecological destruction, Vizenor's haiku present constructive principles that may, like teachings of the Good Life, illuminate the reader's understanding of how everyday sightings of the more-than-human world emphasize basic but important truths about living communities.

One way that Vizenor's haiku share similarities with principles of the Good Life is in how they seek knowledge from the more-than-human world. By describing the perspectives of the other-than-human, the haiku suggest a way to attempt to understand how their motivations and behaviors fit into a larger picture. A poem in Seventeen Chirps reads,

> Maple beetle
> Stood where I was writing
> Watching the cat (n.p.).

From a human perspective, the situation seems quite ordinary. The speaker's writing activity might be momentarily interrupted by the appearance of a beetle. One human response could be to sweep the beetle away and continue writing. However, the speaker notes the dynamics of the situation from the perspective of the beetle, whose attention is focused on the cat—perhaps warily. Even though there is nothing surprising in the idea that an insect would focus its attention on a cat, perhaps out of a sense of self-preservation, it is unusual to conceive of everyday confrontations with the more-than-human world from the perspective of the insect that interrupts one's work. Vizenor's shift in perspective in the scene suggests a different way to regard the ordinary world in order to learn from the other-than-human.

Vizenor's haiku often express this dynamic by using small, common animals found in North American urban or rural environments as subjects. Thomas Lynch notes that this use of small creatures as subject matter is a characteristic found in both Japanese Edo period haiku (1603–1867) and the Anishinaabe oral tradition. Lynch states that "[b]oth haiku and tribal literatures take the tiniest of creatures seriously for their own sake, not for what . . . they might be made to symbolize of the human condition" (211). According to Haruo Shirane, the poetry of the Edo period introduced subjects "taken from everyday commoner life and reflect[ing] popular culture in both the cities and the countryside" (176). Insects were a popular haiku subject, their sounds in poetry symbolizing the passing of the seasons, while their short lives exemplified the Buddhist sense of impermanence (Shirane 180). Shirane has a different perspective than Lynch on the role of insects in Japanese haiku, finding that poems about insects also "reflect a larger cultural fascination with and sympathy for small creatures . . . which function as metaphors for the condition of low-level commoners and farmers" (181). Regardless, much of Edo period haiku focuses on the more-than-human world, often aiming to stir empathy for or realizations about the larger world through a study of the very small. While these ideas share similarities with the wisdom to be gained from learning to live from the more-than-human world, in accordance with the teachings of the Good Life, it is not quite the same thing, as some of the forthcoming comparisons between Vizenor's haiku and the Edo poets to whom he responds will demonstrate. Vizenor's haiku are less concerned with compassion than with inquiring into animal subjectivities, indicating, in a manner like ideas of the Good Life, how insight is to be gained from trying to see the world from the perspective of the other-than-human. Blaeser notes that Vizenor's haiku offer "illuminating twists on the way we perceive ourselves" and challenge "our overserious or isolationist view of our actions" (128). As with Vizenor's dark portrayal of a postapocalyptic future in his novel *Bearheart*, his haiku persistently challenge an objectified version of nature and the limitations of the human perspective. However, the haiku are presented in a lighthearted manner that offers the reader a novel or uplifting experience, much like Edo period haiku expressing the joy and humor in Zen philosophy.

A comparison between Japanese Edo period haiku and Vizenor's haiku clarifies how Vizenor responds to the haiku scenes that seem to have inspired his nature haiku. Vizenor has frequently mentioned Matsuo Bashō, Yosa Buson, and Kobayashi Issa in his writing about haiku. In the introduction to his haiku book *Cranes Arise*, Vizenor states that his poems "tease the memories of three haiku poets" (para. 7). In the same essay, Vizenor quotes Reginald Blyth, who describes Bashō as religious, Buson as artistic, and Issa as humanistic (para. 8). In *Postindian Conversations*, Vizenor suggests how the poets contribute to own poetic identity with the use of animal imagery in declaring that "Bashō is . . . a teaser of seasons, and an imagistic philosopher of impermanence. Issa . . . teased the birds and worried insects in his nature . . . Bashō was a water strider. Issa was a sparrow. Buson was a crane in the mirror. I was a crane, a cedar waxwing, a bear" ("Postindian" 33). These comments suggest Vizenor's association of Edo period poets with small animals as well as his own identification with certain animals from a tribal perspective. Similar to how Edo period haiku observe and sympathize with small and subtle aspects of nature, Vizenor's haiku urge the reader to take the animal's perspective in the scene, as observed in the poem described previously. In the poem, the shift from the writer observing the beetle to the beetle observing the cat nudges the reader to consider the multiple perspectives in the scene, which in turn reveals other dynamics at play beyond those related to typical human concerns. Vizenor's responses to and transformations of Edo period haiku express three important qualities: Vizenor's use of minute details and perspectives that often elude human notice, the ways that other-than-human creatures use and share spaces, and the close relationship between artistic creation and the more-than-human world.

Small Details

Bashō is a poet often mentioned in Vizenor's writings about haiku. Some of Vizenor's descriptions of Bashō emphasize Bashō's pursuit of religious and philosophical truths through writing nature poetry. Quoting from Makoto Ueda's *Bashō and His Interpreters* in his introduction to *Cranes Arise*, Vizenor notes that Bashō chose *fuga*, an artist's way of life, in pursuit of an eternal truth in nature (para. 10). Vizenor also quotes Ueda's passages about Bashō's last days of life, including Bashō's final haiku evoking his illness and suffering and his wry comments about the flies' interest in the presence of his ailing body (*Cranes*, para. 11). Vizenor's attention to this passage from Ueda highlights the attention that Bashō gives to the perspectives of animals. Some of Vizenor's haiku mention Bashō (and other Edo period poets) by name, incorporating the poet into his own haiku scenes. One of Vizenor's poems recalls a haiku for which Bashō is well-known but includes the poet himself into the scene. Like Bashō's haiku, Vizenor's emphasizes the behavior or perspective of the other-than-human. Vizenor's translation of Bashō's poem reads,

SEVEN

> an ancient pond,
> a frog jumps in,
> sound of water ("Envoy" 60).

Vizenor writes,

> calm in the storm
> master bashō soaks his feet
> water striders ("Envoy" 60).

Iadonisi considers the subversive undertones in Vizenor's poem, noting that "[a]s Vizenor acknowledges Bashō's greatness by bestowing on him the title 'master,' Vizenor audaciously crafts a new narrative, one in which the Japanese master is in the pond while insects skitter on the surface" (71). Even as Vizenor reconstructs the peaceful silence of the poet at the pond, the presence of the haiku "master" is used to emphasize, ironically, the ordinariness of humans. However, reading the poem with respect to the philosophy of the Good Life, particularly regarding the importance of studying the world from the perspective of the other-than-human, the poem is also subversive in countering the logocentric hierarchy of humans over nonhumans. In Vizenor's poem, Bashō, a human, becomes an object to contemplate, especially by way of contrast to the water striders, whose very different anatomy enables them to walk across the water's surface.

The poem, like many of Vizenor's haiku, leaves room for interpretation, simply placing Bashō and the water striders together and inviting the reader to draw conclusions about the pairing. Vizenor has experimented with the idea of a haiku "envoy" to explain the significance of his haiku in prose. Vizenor defines the "envoy" as "a discourse on the reach of haiku sensations and tribal survivance" ("Envoy" 60). While the majority of Vizenor's haiku are presented without accompanying envoys, these envoys also appear occasionally in his other writings, such as his novel *Hiroshima Bugi: Atomu 57*, to direct the reader's interpretation of a scene. The metacommentary the envoys provide seem to offer guidance toward interpretations of Vizenor's creative work, a move which, in the case of Vizenor's statements on his own haiku, Lynch questions as "possible authorial interpretive hegemony, alien to the haiku spirit" (216). On the other hand, the envoys, with their lyrical qualities, could be interpreted as part of the creative work itself, as in the case of the example that follows. Regardless, the comments in the envoys, as Lynch's observation suggests, leave less room for interpretation than the haiku themselves and do possess a certain instructive quality. This instructive quality seems to nudge the reader to consider the human's position in community with the more-than-human world and to view such communities from other-than-human perspectives. The envoy that Vizenor provides for the poem above, for instance, favors animals' experiences and perspectives in stating, "[t]he striders listen to the wind, the creation of sound that is heard and seen in the motion of water; the wind teases the tension and natural balance on the surface of the world. The same wind that moves the spiders teases the poets" ("Envoy" 31). The envoy emphasizes the connections between nonhuman animals, wind, water, and humans. Furthermore, Vizenor's envoy more clearly reveals the perspective of the water striders, who experience the subtleties of wind as it ripples across the water's surface to a much greater degree than a human normally would. This attention to the small and subtle movements in a natural scene suggests a way of learning from the more-than-human world, of conceiving of a living community from multiple perspectives and appreciating how different individuals affect one other.

The idea expressed in this haiku envoy of centering nonhuman viewpoints in a scene may be applied to Vizenor's other haiku. Like the Edo period poets that inspire him, Vizenor focuses on the small and the common. Vizenor's attraction to haiku as a literary mode to describe nature in a way that effectively counters Western anthropocentric viewpoints is understandable, as well as his close identification to Bashō and other Edo period poets, given their similar values. Bashō's expression of Zen Buddhist ideologies through haiku have much in common with Vizenor's ethic toward the environment in their portrayal of animal subjectivities and attention to details of a natural scene normally lost on the casual human observer. For instance, in *Seventeen Chirps*, Vizenor writes,

> Ahead in my path
> The grasshoppers jumped one by one
> Shaking the oak leaves (n.p.).

While the jumping of grasshoppers is easy for the human to perceive, the effects of their movements on surrounding vegetation is a subtle detail that could escape the human observer's notice. Certain details in the poem are magnified, suggesting how the jumping of grasshoppers and shaking of leaves could seem from the perspective of a much smaller creature. With a new awareness of how these small and subtle movements fall beneath our notice, we might begin to perceive the world in a different way, through the eyes of the small, common, other-than-human creatures that surround us on a daily basis.

The haiku scenes in many of Vizenor's poems emphasize the importance of connections between individuals, human and nonhuman, within a community, and how individuals affect one another. This community includes the poet, who is not an impartial observer, but a person sharing experiences with other persons in the scene. While this idea is by no means unique to Vizenor's haiku, it is a prominent feature of his poetry. Blaeser, observing how Vizenor draws on multiple traditions for his haiku, notes that "[t]he distinction between observing and being-engaged-in is key in Zen and in a Native American perspective of life and literature, for the idea of beholding nature automatically creates a division and sets up a subject/object relationship that makes of nature thing, not being" (125). One way that Vizenor's haiku actively resist this subject/object relationship is in their emphasis on small details that inspire the reader to consider how the other-than-human would view the scene, emphasizing that the human perspective of the world is only one of many. Vizenor's haiku often return to the perspective of small creatures, inquiring why and how they go about their business in the world. While such poems, read in isolation, may impress the reader with their novelty, a persuasive quality emerges across a volume of Vizenor's haiku due to this consistent presentation of small details and other-than-human perspectives.

As humans, we tend to be attentive to the details that concern ourselves and tend to conceive of ourselves as the architects of structure and order in the world. However, the small details of Vizenor's haiku at times describe the effects achieved by nonhuman creators. For instance, in

> Spider threads
> Held the red sumac still
> Autumn wind (*Seventeen*)

the haiku scene describes a subtle detail from everyday life—that of how a spider's web immobilizes the leaves of a tree, preventing them from rustling in the wind. By bringing notice to this minor, not uncommon sight, the poem reinforces the ideas prevailing throughout many of Vizenor's haiku: details, connections between disparate living things, and the agential power of nonhumans. In exploring nonhuman agency, Vizenor's haiku focus on how nonhuman creatures inhabit, utilize, and share their surroundings.

How Other-than-Human Creatures Use Spaces

In addition to Bashō, Buson is mentioned in Vizenor's writings as an important source of inspiration. In the introduction to *Cranes Arise*, Vizenor quotes Donald Keene's description of Buson's poetry and visual artistry, stating that "in 'Buson's poetry, as in his paintings, realistic description was of little importance when compared to the nobility of the conception'" (*Cranes* para. 13). Along similar lines, Ueda notes that "Buson brought to his verse a painter's eye for form and color, along with an expansive imagination and a taste for the exotic, which at times led him to portray people and events remote in time or space" (Ueda 6). Buson's poem,

> winter rain
> a mouse runs
> over the koto

translated in the introduction of Vizenor's *Favor of Crows*, describes music resulting from the scurrying of a mouse over a traditional Japanese stringed instrument (xvi). The poem reflects the comments of Keene and Ueda in its portrayal of an image or idea that is more interesting in concept than realistic. While it is interesting to imagine the idea of music produced unintentionally by a collision between mouse and a stringed instrument, the scene itself is not an everyday one. Vizenor's response to this work suggests how in addition to the use of small and subtle details from everyday life, described in the preceding section, his haiku use scenarios unusual or even impossible for humans to observe to convey the experiences and perspectives of nonhumans. Vizenor reframes elements of Buson's haiku with

> cold rain
> field mice rattle the dishes
> buson's koto (*Favor* xvi).

Like Buson, Vizenor begins the poem by mentioning the cold weather, striking a contrast between the warmth and security of the home and its chilly surroundings. In Vizenor's poem, the mice, instead of producing music through incidental contact with the stringed instrument, are presumably trying to scavenge bits of food from used dishes in a sink. Vizenor juxtaposes the image with that of Buson's by simply referencing the former as "buson's koto" (*Favor* xvi). In contrast to Buson's haiku, Vizenor's suggests some rationale for the mice's behavior. Thus, rather than producing an intriguing or unusual scenario for the reader to contemplate, the poem leaves the reader to consider the reason for the mice's presence in the home as well as their aim. Similarly to Vizenor's image of Bashō, soaking his feet alongside the very differently embodied water striders, the lines take inspiration from the famous haiku to create a different kind of effect, one that emphasizes the other-than-human presence in the scene. Rather than the startling effect of music from the animal's interaction with an instrument, the scene focuses attention on how and why the mice have breached the human dwelling, privileging their interests over the aesthetic their presence produces.

Other haiku by Vizenor emphasize animals' use of humans' everyday spaces, providing insight into these spaces from a perspective sympathetic to the concerns of the other-than-human. In

> The song sparrows
> Nested in the choir loft
> Six days a week (*Seventeen*)

the speaker draws attention to a space only periodically used by humans to consider how its animal inhabitants make use of it on all but church-going days. We may know on some level that we share our spaces with uninvited other-than-human guests, some more of a nuisance than others, but consciousness of this fact tends to elude us—perhaps because it is troubling or because it does not concern us. Vizenor's haiku often highlight that which does not concern us to demonstrate other ways to see our surroundings as well as to depict how our behaviors affect other-than-human creatures. For instance, on church-going days, the sparrows must flee from their accustomed home, perhaps leaving hatchlings behind, until the humans have left the building. The haiku scene emphasizes an ordinary situation that might otherwise escape our notice, one that questions our concept of "vacant" spaces. Often, spaces vacated by humans are, after all, readily inhabited by the other-than-human. This emphasis on how living creatures, including humans, affect one another, is heightened in

> The bridge spider
> Once the birds began to nest
> Moved into the bell (*Seventeen*).

In this poem, the spider, threatened by the presence of birds moving into one human-made space, relocates to another human-made space to elude the potential predators. We are surrounded by shadowed, little-seen spaces where small creatures make their homes. This comes to our attention when we walk into spider webs or lift a rock only to find a tiny community. The spider's future is uncertain—will it find a peaceful existence within the shelter of the bell, or will its new attempt to make a living be destroyed by the bell's ringing? While the scene could be imagined in many different ways, it provokes us to ask how we affect the small creatures who try to dwell in spaces or objects we consider to be our own, or how other-than-humans view or use human-made objects in line with their own purposes.

To the Western logocentric perspective, humans alone are the possessors of rational thought. However, the Anishinaabe philosophy of the Good Life does not emphasize this idea, since it is not necessarily useful for learning to live in community with others. Instead, humans are required to validate their importance as persons by proving their ability to learn from the more-than-human world. Other-than-human creatures engage with the world according to their own purposes, revealing different perspectives and approaches. According to the Good Life, we are destined not to be the only "rational" beings but instead to grow in wisdom about the communities of humans and nonhumans that surround us by learning from all living things. Vizenor's haiku align with this idea in how they focus on details in a natural scene that emphasize the perspectives of the other-than-human and consider how other-than-human creatures occupy and share spaces with other beings. Vizenor's haiku also explore the boundaries and definitions of art, including the art of haiku, to emphasize the creative powers of the other-than-human.

Other-than-Human Arts

Another Edo period poet of importance in Vizenor's writings is Kobayashi Issa. Vizenor describes Issa as a humanist by nature, a sentiment echoed in Ueda's comment that Issa "wrote some powerful and intensely personal haiku" (6). Vizenor notes in particular that Issa "is moved by nature" and "includes references to his presence in haiku scenes" (*Favor* xxii). In terms of Vizenor's own critique of a logocentric perspective, his admiration for this quality in Issa's work aligns with his own tendency to question or subvert the centrality of the human perspective in his haiku. By incorporating his own presence as a part of the natural scene, Issa suggests an idea similar to Vizenor's that humans are in community with other animals, the human perspective only one of many to be considered and understood. Vizenor writes of Issa that "[t]he frogs continue to croak his name, skinny Issa in the secret marsh, and he is celebrated everywhere by crickets, mosquitoes, flies, many insects, and many birds in the voices of nature and survivance" (*Favor* xxxi). Vizenor's comment suggests that Issa's ability to empathize with other beings, reflected in his haiku, has earned him respect and affection from the kinds of small, vulnerable animals his poems describe.

Many of Vizenor's own haiku share this quality of Issa's sympathy for small creatures, although Vizenor's sympathies are expressed by centering the perceptions and concerns of the creatures themselves rather than a particular human perspective. Vizenor responds to a haiku of Issa's in a manner similar to his responses to Bashō and Buson, first sharing a translation of Issa's poem

SEVEN

> skinny frog
> don't be discouraged
> issa is here (*Favor* xxii).

Issa's haiku demonstrates Vizenor's observations on his style in indicating the poet's presence as part of the natural scene, Issa's identification with the "skinny frog" suggesting the poet's own feeling of lack or discouragement. Vizenor responds to Issa's poem with

> tricky frogs
> croak a haiku in the marsh
> skinny issa (*Favor* xxiii).

Vizenor's haiku communicates a particular homage to Issa's concern with small creatures while also suggesting that these creatures have their own poetry to share with humans. The haiku portrays a kind of haiku that emerges directly from a nonhuman source — a haiku within a haiku. Vizenor's haiku is not only human-mediated but responsive to a canonical haiku text, which is a logocentric practice, while the haiku his own poem describes is mediated through nonhumans. Vizenor's response to Buson's haiku previously described also relates to this idea of reimagining canonical haiku scenes in new poems. Vizenor's scene of mice scurrying through dishes next to "buson's koto" strives toward an unembellished portrayal of the more-than-human world (*Favor* xvi). The final line of Vizenor's poem gestures to the contrast between Buson's idealistic portrayal and Vizenor's more realistic scene, which focuses on the natural behavior of the mice, rather than the effect their movements produce on human senses. However, artistic realism, in the sense of copying the reality of our human senses, is not necessarily the effect for which Vizenor's poetry strives. Vizenor's novel *Hiroshima Bugi* describes an idea of haiku as emerging from the spiritual part of nature, providing further insight into what Vizenor may mean in describing the haiku expressions of frogs.

In *Hiroshima Bugi,* the protagonist Ronin, of Anishinaabe and Japanese descent, reflects on his childhood discovery of haiku poetry through an encounter with water spirits called *nanazu*, near Sagami Bay, Japan. The "water tricksters," described as "curious, moist, miniature humans . . . nude, bluish at the creases," tease the seven-year-old Ronin (27). Nori, one of the nanazu, instructs Ronin "to shout out three natural words to create a poem, a new world of perfect memory" (29). However, when Ronin constructs an image of his found wooden sword as an ocean bounty, Nori objects to the poem, telling him that the sword was a gift of the nanazu, "the tricksters of rivers and ocean waves" (29). Nori's critique implies that Ronin's perception of the scene is false because it fails to acknowledge the role of other sentient beings in its creation. This account of haiku indicates an idea like that which has been described throughout this essay—that Vizenor's haiku center on various connections between different beings. The falseness in Ronin's poem comes from its description of the wooden sword as an object, rather than a source of connection between himself and the nanazu. If this scene is taken to reflect Vizenor's own beliefs about creating poetry, it suggests that Vizenor conceives of haiku as a way to emphasize the presences and perspectives of others that elude ordinary human perceptions, as well as how Vizenor's understanding of haiku itself comes from learning from the more-than-human world.

Although Ronin's childhood poem falls short because of his short-sightedness toward the connections between different beings, he ultimately develops understanding of haiku creation through observing Nori's creation of a haiku. Nori shouts "three words into the crotch of a tree . . . and then, at a great distance, a voice repeated three scenes of an imagistic haiku poem," whereupon Ronin hears the poem,

> ancient pond
> the nanazu leap
> sound of water (*Hiroshima* 29).

SEVEN

In addition to generating this particular appropriation of Bashō's poem described earlier in the essay, Nori instructs Ronin to "[t]hrow cucumbers into the water when [his] visions and dance of words are about to vanish in the undertow of a crowd" as a way to attract the nanazu to his aid (*Hiroshima* 29). Thus, according to the account of haiku described in *Hiroshima Bugi*, the nanazu, rather than humans, are the true experts and teachers of clear, imagistic language. *Hiroshima Bugi* suggests an understanding of haiku as rooted firmly in knowledge gathered from the workings of nature, particularly in its use of the nanazu, spiritual beings that stand outside of Western logocentric concepts of nature.

Similarly, the playful imagery of the "tricky frogs" provokes us to reconsider our understanding of artistic creation. This notion of nonhumans as teachers connects not only to the philosophy of the Good Life but also the Japanese belief in *kami*, the idea that all living things have a potential divinity. Noting that all beings present at a *matsuri*, or sacred festival, become divine, Hoshinaga Fumio states that "[a]ll living things can be(come) *kami* . . . Of course—actually a dragonfly, a frog—do not join their hands in prayer; yet they are within the sacred locale of the festival" (Gilbert 168-169). Just as Vizenor's tribute to Issa poses frogs as the creators of haiku, the following from *Cranes Arise*,

> *grand marais, minnesota*
> downy woodpecker
> beats a tune on a dead tree
> superior sonata (n.p.)

describes a relatively common sound with high praise. While playful, the poem contrasts human and animal capabilities similarly to Vizenor's poem of Bashō and the water striders. In Western logocentric thinking, the human is always superior to the animal; thus, animals are defined in the human mind by their limitations, rather than their special capabilities. In the poem, Vizenor rethinks this hierarchy by describing the woodpecker's distinctive sounds with terms of praise reserved for human musicians. The precision and rapidity of movement, for instance, for which a human virtuoso might strive, is effortless to this very different animal and is, in fact, a very ordinary behavior for them. The poem might provoke us to reconsider the limitations of our own bodies and our assumptions of superiority over the other-than-human based on what we perceive as our intellectual and artistic achievements. Vizenor's haiku communicate beliefs in the sacred nature of the more-than-human world and the divine qualities of the other-than-human. At the same time, these haiku scenes are very straightforward in their presentation, calling on the reader's knowledge of animal behavior to complete the idea. Vizenor's haiku imply that nature's artists and teachers are all around us, and no special abilities are needed to perceive their expressions.

Over the decades, while Vizenor's haiku have consistently expressed notions of other-than-human subjectivities and a subordinate human role in the universe, the style of his haiku has changed, querying the boundaries and potential connections between devices from the English language and the qualities of Japanese haiku. Ross notes that "English haiku normally uses punctuation marks in much the same way" as the *kireji*, or cutting word, in Japanese haiku, indicating a pause or stop (xiii). Vizenor's earlier haiku used both capitalization and punctuation, as can be seen in the poems quoted from *Seventeen Chirps*. In his most recent haiku book, *Favor of Crows*, Vizenor eliminates capitalization and punctuation, which gives the poems a more ethereal, disembodied quality and distances them from the English language's manner of indicating structure and order. An earlier book, *Cranes Arise*, shows an even more significant departure from English-language haiku conventions in including a place name in italics before the three lines of the haiku, as exemplified in the above haiku, which notes the location of the scene as "*grand marais, minnesota*" (*Cranes*, n.p.). Vizenor does not explain this change in his haiku in his introduction to *Cranes Arise*; however, the additional line has an effect like that of his haiku envoy of explaining—or even over-explaining, in the spirit of Lynch's observation on the haiku envoy—the haiku setting. Applied throughout the book, the additional line has a documentarian quality that increases the reader's awareness of Vizenor's role in describing the scene and orients the haiku in a specific reality to a higher degree than his other haiku collections without the place name. However, in considering Vizenor's overall aim in haiku, the place name may not function so much to document reality but to remind the reader of the embodied experience of the haiku scene.

As considered previously in the essay, English-language haiku have, according to Ross, Giroux, and other scholars, often struggled against the Western linguistic and ideological constraints that prevent the kind of direct, radiant expression English speakers consider ideal in Japanese haiku. However, while Vizenor's haiku often economize on words and express a haiku moment, as Blaeser has noted, after the fashion of Japanese haiku, his experiments with the envoy and the additional line in *Cranes Arise* imply that producing haiku in the Japanese tradition is less a priority than directing the reader's attention to various qualities of his work. These devices attest to the way that Vizenor's haiku instruct the reader to observe material reality in a specific way. As a means of communicating the more-than-human world to the reader in a manner of instruction like the Good Life, Vizenor's haiku prioritize communicating a challenging but compelling lens for interpreting the natural world over fidelity to the haiku form or to the conventions of English-language haiku.

Conclusion

Vizenor's haiku communicate a particular perspective of living with a deepened awareness of the more-than-human world, in a manner like mino-bimaadiziwin, the Anishinaabe philosophy of the Good Life. Three recurring qualities in Vizenor's haiku that communicate this perspective are a focus on small details relevant to other-than-human lives; how other-than-human creatures utilize and share spaces with others, including humans; and how artistic creations, sometimes mediated by humans, ultimately emerge from the more-than-human world. While Vizenor's poetry has clearly taken inspiration from the Japanese haiku tradition, in responding to poets Matsuo Bashō, Yosa Buson, and Kobayashi Issa, his poems emphasize different aspects of familiar haiku scenes that provide further insight into the more-than-human world, as well as our own very limited human perspective in it.

In many other literary works, such as his novel *Bearheart*, Vizenor has critiqued Western logocentricity for its destructive effects on human and animal lives. While Vizenor's haiku disavow Western rational definitions of life and community, they also exemplify the development of one's knowledge about the more-than-human world through viewing ordinary sights in the natural world, offering a constructive perspective on the issue. Instead of describing human feelings and responses to nature, Vizenor's haiku provoke readers to consider the world through different eyes, engaging an ethic of respect for and community with the natural world.

Many of Vizenor's haiku pose the experiences of other-than-human beings as important sources of knowledge for living in community with others, thus sharing certain teachings of the Good Life.

Works Cited

Abram, David. *The Spell of the Sensuous: Perception and Language in a More-than-Human World*. Vintage, 1996.

—. *Becoming Animal: An Earthly Cosmology*. Vintage, 2011.

Blaeser, Kimberly. "Multiple Traditions in Haiku." *Gerald Vizenor: Writing in the Oral Tradition*. University of Oklahoma Press, 1996, pp. 108-135.

Burns, Allan. Introduction. *Where the River Goes: The Nature Tradition in English-Language Haiku.* Snapshot Press, 2013, pp. 9-68.

Debassige, Brent. "Re-conceptualizing Anishinaabe Mino-Bimaadiziwin (the Good Life) as Research Methodology: A Spirit-centered Way in Anishinaabe Research." *Canadian Journal of Native Education*, vol. 33, no. 1, 2010, pp. 11-28.

Dreese, Donelle N. *Ecocriticism: Creating Self and Place in Environmental and American Indian Literatures.* Peter Lang Publishing, Inc., 2002.

Gilbert, Richard. "Hoshinaga Fumio." *Poems of Consciousness: Contemporary Japanese & English-Language Haiku in Cross-Cultural Perspective.* Red Moon Press, 2008, pp. 161-196.

Giroux, Joan. *The Haiku Form.* Tuttle, 1974.

Iadonisi, Richard A. "Gerald Vizenor's 'Socioacupuncture' through His Haiku." *Journal of Ethnic American Literature*, vol. 3, 2013, pp. 64-86.

Keene, Donald, editor. *Anthology of Japanese Literature.* Grove Press, 1955.

Kruse, Marc, Nicholas Tanchuk, and Robert Hamilton. "Educating in the Seventh Fire: Debewewin, Mino-Bimaadiziwin, and Ecological Justice. *Educational Theory*, vol. 69, no. 5, 2019, pp. 587-601.

Lynch, Thomas. "To Honor Impermanence: The Haiku and Other Poems of Gerald Vizenor." *Loosening the Seams: Interpretations of Gerald Vizenor*, ed. A. Robert Lee, Bowling Green State University Popular Press, 2000, pp. 203-224.

Ross, Bruce, ed. Introduction. *Haiku Moment: An Anthology of Contemporary North American Haiku*. Tuttle, 1993.

Shirane, Haruo. *Japan and the Culture of the Four Seasons*. Columbia UP, 2012.

Ueda, Makoto. "Introduction." *Modern Japanese Poets and the Nature of Literature*. Stanford UP, 1983, pp. 1-8.

Vizenor, Gerald. *Cranes Arise*. Nodin Press, 1999.

—. "The Envoy to Haiku." *Chicago Review,* vol. 39, no. 3/4, A North Pacific Rim Reader, 1993, pp. 55-62.

—. *Favor of Crows*. Wesleyan UP, 2014.

—. *Hiroshima Bugi: Atomu 57*. University of Nebraska Press, 2003.

— and A. Robert Lee. *Postindian Conversations*. University of Nebraska Press, 1999.

—. *Seventeen Chirps*. Nodin Press, 1964.

Poet/Artist: Amiri Baraka

The Haiku In Amiri Baraka's Low Coup

CRYSTAL SIMONE SMITH

ABSTRACT: Prolific poet and founder of the Black Arts Movement, Amiri Baraka, developed and maintained an abiding interest in Asian culture throughout his polarizing career. In his 1984 memoir, The Autobiography of LeRoi Jones/Amiri Baraka, he recalls himself as a young man "transported by the hundreds of scholarly books on various schools of Buddhism and Eastern thought." Specifically, he mentioned R.H. Blythe's books on Zen and one of the four volumes of Haiku (1949-1952). These were likely his first encounters with Zen and haiku.

Though fascinated with Zen, Baraka was widely known for his use of poetic forms as critical indictments of racism and "the ruling class." In the late 1990s, Baraka began engaging with haiku, inventing his own hybrid form inspired by the Japanese form. He called his version "low coup," often describing the politically charged anti-odes as "like haiku, but different." His micro-poems replaced Zen with satire and fury, thus it seemed logical to dismiss any authentic connections between the forms. For nearly a decade, he held jazz-accompanied readings and published two collections of "low coup" underscoring his complex engagement with Asian cultural traditions and his ongoing commitment to racial justice through resistance.

To open a low coup reading, Amiri Baraka presented his audience with a brief explanation of the invented form: "It's like haiku but it's different." It was more caveat than definition and his stance was clear; low coup would not simply embody picturesque nature scenes or those sudden moments of enlightenment indicative of contemporary English-language haiku poets. It would further explore the deeper-meaning concepts specific to culture and structural racism, and reflect his resolute, radical thoughts on those issues.

Known for his improvisatory approach to poetic forms and performances, of the form low coup he once joked, "Black people are too lazy to count syllables." Thus, he replaced "low" for "hai" –high and "ku" was replaced with "coup" to imply a rebellious uprising (Rambsy 1). While contemporary English-language haiku is not bounded to syllable counting, it does challenge the poet to achieve good haiku through a set of stylistic elements that includes sensory images, brevity, and tension. Alluding to these elements, Baraka begin writing low coup in the late nineties. Though renowned for his political free verse, low coup deconstructed and condensed the monumental subjects of revolution and racial injustice into micro-poems. A decades-long advocate of racial consciousness, to simplify was the way to clarity for Baraka as he believed most racism was based on false theories and the applications of social labels.

Taking into consideration the aforementioned description, some common areas of interests can be explored in Baraka's low coup in relation to contemporary haiku. In *Haiku and Senryu: A Simple Guide for All*, author Charlotte Digregorio describes the process of writing haiku as collectively capturing "our awe of nature, and our consciousness of being a small part of it, that others can relate to" (Digregorio 12). Awareness, or pointedly, a raised consciousness, permeates Baraka's low coup. Though he appears to reject the nuances of haiku form, he deftly achieves Digregorio's process in the following low coup.

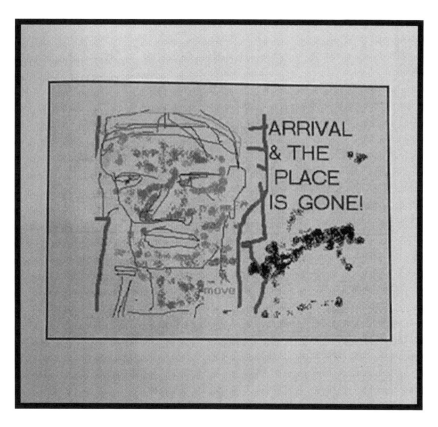

move

arrival
& the place
is gone!

While it is less concerned with nature, we can relate to going beyond one's familiarity or environment seeking engagement in another. With the disappointment of what's no longer present, there's also a hinting or awareness to the socio-economical aspects of Black upward mobility or gentrification.

The "move" low coup above opens his collection entitled, *Un Poco Low Coup* (2004), of twenty-four poems interspersed with

Black folk art. Many of the poems are titled with a word or phrase integral to the poem's context. Considered the Godfather of The Black Arts Movement and a vastly influential, controversial figure, Baraka was committed to artistic innovation often mapping and intersecting visual art, music—in particular jazz—and poetry. The title incorporates Bud Powell's jazz tune, Un Poco Loco, a translation that means "A Little Crazy" –used as a denotation to the psychosis of racism. In his reading performances of low coup, the tune was often played in accompaniment by a jazz ensemble situated behind the poet, keeping time. If no band was present, Baraka would hum bits of it between poems. Many of the poems are titled with some variation of "low coup." In the title poem below, we are called to act, to rebel

against systematic oppression by the author, who was considered by peer artists and others "a public poet, an agitator" (Gery, 167) As a revolutionist, there was almost an absence of rational within him that was noticeable to his followers.

> **low coup**
>
> craziness is no act
> not to act
> is crazinezzzzz

As a transfixing voice of resistance, it is likely Baraka was also drawn to haiku because of the tension, a fundamental aesthetic of haiku. It is the tension that taps the reader's imagination and fully engages h/er in the poem. It is a restraint created by the juxtaposition of two concepts or images. The two create an implication or space that hints at the significance. Though, low coup creates this space in certain ways, the hint is often intentionally less subtle. Baraka never failed to be resounding in the room, even his silence and candor were piercing as apparent in the following low coup.

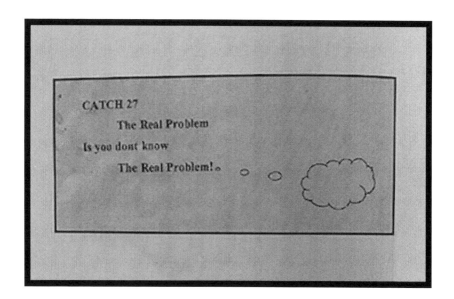

SEVEN

Catch 27

The real problem
Is you don't know
The real problem!

The juxtaposition in "Catch 27" appears to imply racists possess no distinct understanding of the syndrome thus suggesting that racism is an unresolvable or uncurable condition. "Catch 27" is also a proclamation with the unabashed use of "you" referencing and contesting a white audience that goes beyond the boundaries of his Black counterparts to create an explicit universal dialogue.

Scholar Michael Dylan Welch, writes: "In moving from private vision (initial experience or impression) to public vision, haiku go through a process of crafting and revision, transforming the particular into the universal, and of becoming fit for consumption" (Welch 1). Baraka achieves this in his low coup only it is a universal experience that is distinctive to Black culture. As an intellectual and scholar, Baraka remained an unapologetic speaker of Black English. In poetry, plays, and performances, the Black vernacular reverberated through his work with a glittering playfulness or sharp slashing of structural oppression. The informal grammar and slang were intended to build an intimacy that formulated a legitimacy with Black listeners. This solidarity with audiences was crucial for radical poets in order to awaken the consciousness of the black masses. With use of these practices, low coup resonated broadly with his audiences. The wit and punchlines landed like daggers in the following poems.

low coup for Bush 2

the main thing
wrong with you
is you ain't in jail

culture

european jews
say the devil
speak perfect German

black americans
on the other hand say, he speak
pretty good english too!

The poet emphasizes the collective attitudes of Blacks in a call for, then-President Bush II, to pay for his alleged war crimes. In "culture," which is a two-part poem I have written as a haiku sequence, the poet revives the myth of the White man in devil form as he compares and connects the persecutions of both ethnic groups.

Recurrently, in live performances, the audiences responded in riotous agreement to his satirical critique of racial relations in America. The dramatic reading accompanied by lively jazz could be misconstrued as passive, reducing the nation's racial failures and brutalization of Black people to political jokes, though in Baraka's case, a poet of such distinctive voice; the audience appeared to urge his lampooning. The absurdity of the hypocrisy in White oppression warranted the laughter. "Laughing to keep from crying" is a noted adage among the Black community and a sort of social optimism.

Though the act of writing low coup was a practice of rebellion, Baraka's low coup resembles the aesthetics of haiku most when he adopted a tone of solemnity. In principle, haiku is to be present in a moment, to distill that moment. In the following low coups, Baraka creates universal poems that slant more toward haiku than his other low coups.

SEVEN

Animal Scientist

have you ever looked
up at the buildings
then looked up at the sky?

1 + 1 = 1

we are the blues
ourselves
the actual song

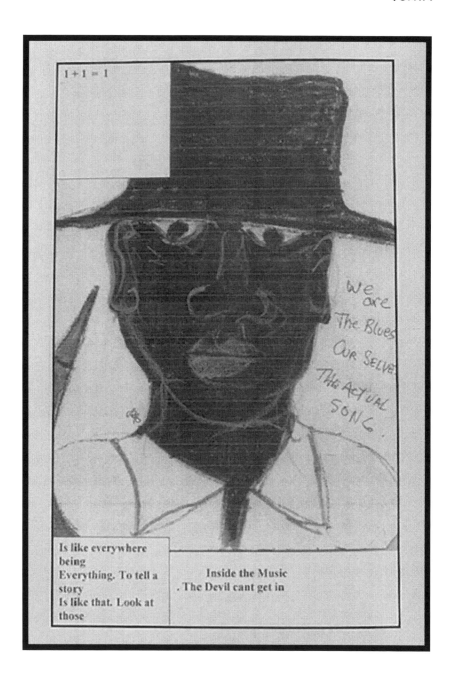

SEVEN

The title "Animal Scientist" is a reference to urban life and the chaos of the city grid, often the zoomorphic comparison of a rat race. In keeping with haiku aesthetics, the poem is more suggestion than statement. It offers two images, one constructed, the other natural. The reader is tasked to consider h/er existence in the bustle of the towering cityscape versus the universe. It also begs the question: Who is in control, commercial forces or God? "1 + 1 = 1" illuminates the harsh, enduring conditions created by the American legacy of White oppression of Blacks while paying tribute to the rich culture of that expression in blues music. The title is a clear indicator that circumstances don't add up equally for Blacks in America.

Finally, there are few articles and definitive criticism focused on Baraka's adaptation of haiku. While Baraka was a goliath among Black poets, in constant observation of the world recording the racial ills that plague Black American life, Un Poco Low Coup and many of his works are out of print. His low coup recordings continue to live online, often dismissed by haiku scholars as the form is absent of the spiritually of Zen. Though, there's little acknowledgement of the raised consciousness, universal reach, and the achievement of tension deriving from the juxtapositions of explicit political statements that his low coups so deftly possess.

Works Cited

Rambsy, H. Notes on Amiri Baraka's Low Coup. Cultural Front, 1 Aug. 2014, www.culturalfront.org/2014/08/notes-on-amiri-barakas-low-coup.html.

Digregorio, Charlotte. Haiku and Senryu, A Simple Guide for All, 2014.

Baraka, Amiri. Un Poco Low Coups. Ishmael Reed Pub. Co., 2004.

Gery, John R. O. "Duplicities of Power: Amiri Baraka's and Lorenzo Thomas's Responses to September 11." African American Review, vol. 44, no. 1-2, 2011, pp. 167–180., doi:10.1353/afa.2011.0030.

Welch, Michael Dylan. Private and Public Vision: Learning Haiku from Joyce Carol Oates, 2016, http://www.graceguts.com/essays/private-and-public-vision-learning-haiku-from-joyce-carol-oates.

Poet/Artist: Amiri Baraka

Reading Classical Chinese Poetry with a Haiku Mind:

A Writing Practice

Jianqing Zheng

ABSTRACT: Reading with a haiku mind can be a writing practice. Bashō's early Chinese-style poems are good examples. His haiku—"In the garden / a sweaty shoe—scent / of chrysanthemum"—echoes a poetic line of a classical Chinese poem: "Back from flower-viewing, the horseshoe is scented." This example shows that Basho had a keen eye for a haiku moment from what he read. This creative reading triggers creative thinking with a purpose to play with the images for creative writing. This essay discusses the use of classical Chinese poetic lines as sources for haiku writing.

In classical Chinese poetry, *jueju* (絕句) is a regulated verse form composed of four lines. It has two patterns: *wujue* (五絕) and *qijue* (七絕). *Wujue* has five characters in each line and *qijue* with seven. Though it is a quatrain, *jueju* challenges a poet to master its variant tonal meters. Similar to *jueju* is another regulated verse form called *lüshi* (律詩), which is the eight-line verse with two patterns: *wulü* (五律) which has five characters in each line and *qilü* (七律) which has seven. One element of *jueju* or *lüshi* is the use of caesura in a line or between the two lines. It functions like a pause for a visual correspondence of the two images for an internal comparison. For example, in this couplet in a *lüshi*-style verse composed by the Tang dynasty poet Bai Juyi (白居易, 772–846)—

風吹古木晴天雨
月照平沙夏夜霜

Wind blowing old trees rain on a fine day,
Moon shining on smooth sand frost of summer night.

—the caesura after the fourth word of each line suggests a visual correspondence between the two parts of the images: the wind rustling the leaves of old trees sounds like rain on a sunny day and the moon shining on the smooth sand looks like the summer night frost.

Another example is the first couplet in a *wujue* verse by Li Po (李白, 701–762), the poet of the Tang dynasty more well-known than his contemporaries to the western readers—

床前明月光
疑是地上霜

Bright moonlight before my bed
Looks like frost on the ground.

—which compares the moonlight to the frost to intensify the loneliness of the poet so that he becomes homesick when he looks up at the moon in the second couplet. The cause-effect relationship between the two lines makes the obvious comparison though it may lose the element of suggestion if we read it with a haiku mind:

> bright moonlight
> before my bed
> frost on the ground

These two examples by Bai Juyi and Li Po show that many poetic lines of classical Chinese poetry read like haiku, and this element might have appealed to Japanese poets of early times. As Haruo Shirane points out, "In the first half of the 1680s, during the Tenna era (1681-84), the haikai world was swept by the 'Chinese style' (*kanshibun-chō*), which not only employed Chinese words and compounds, considered to be haikai words, but also utilized Chinese-style syntax, following the *kundoku* tradition of reading Chinese in a semi-Japanese manner" (60-61).

In a sense, reading classical Chinese poetry with a haiku mind can be a good writing practice. Bashō's early Chinese-style poems are good examples. He found something new as good sources for haiku writing. In other words, classical Chinese poetry may appeal for a haiku moment through the mind's eye so that creative reading can trigger creative thinking with a purpose to play with the images for creative writing. Thus, this reading or thinking practice is also an enlightening experience of a haiku mind in order to find a haiku from the classical Chinese poetic lines.

As the title states, this essay will discuss the use of classical Chinese poetic lines as haiku sources and the focus will mainly be on the lines of five characters. Read this line—

SEVEN

冬嶺秀孤松

Winter ridge shows a lone pine tree

—from a *jueju* verse titled "Four Seasons" (四時) by Gu Kaizhi (顧愷之, 345–406), a poet and painter of the Jin dynasty. This line produces an effect of associative thinking between the cold winter mountains and the loneliness of the pine tree. This line carries an element of accepting the state of loneliness in a large, desolate environment. Also, 秀 means "show, appear, on top of, or taller than" as well as "beauty" in Chinese. This line presents a contrast between the horizontal ridge and the vertical pine tree, evoking loneliness and also reflecting an attitude toward life and self. If we look at this line with a haiku eye, we can rearrange it in three lines to highlight the beauty of loneliness:

> winter ridge
> atop it
> a lonely pine

Many lines in classical Chinese poetry read like one-line haiku. Here's a couplet by Du Fu (杜甫, 712–770), a famous poet of the Tang dynasty:

日月籠中鳥
乾坤水上萍

Sun and moon birds in the cage.
Sky and earth duckweeds in the water.

One possible interpretation is that the abstract meaning of 日月 is year after year and that of 乾坤 is everywhere. However, I think since these words are images themselves, they should reflect Du Fu's view of the universe and himself with their original meanings. Each line has two parts of images with an invisible pause after the

141

second word for an internal comparison, a technique widely used in haiku as well. What Du Fu really suggested is that if his miserable life was like a caged bird, so were the sun and the moon, and if he had to wander like drifting duckweed, so did the sky and the earth. With this metaphoric comparison and this visual correspondence between the smallness of a human existence to the largeness of the space, loneliness is everywhere and exists in everything. This couplet, therefore, shows that Du Fu's imagination pervades the universe. In dialectical thinking, loneliness is no longer loneliness. In further reading, this couplet offers us a chance to practice one-line haiku and to notice the caesura in a line for the juxtaposition of the two parts of images which, as Harold G. Henderson analyzed, "are compared to each other, not in simile or metaphor, but as two phenomena, each of which exists in its own right. This may be called 'the principle of internal comparison' in which the differences are just as important as the likenesses" (18).

In classical Chinese poetry, juxtaposition is an important element, which requires a perfect symmetrical contrast of images in a couplet. If the first line is on human nature, the second one is on nature, or vice versa, as shown in the following couplet by the Tang dynasty poet Lu Lun (盧倫, 739 – 799):

歲去人頭白
秋來樹葉黃

Year's end the man's hair whitens
Autumnal arrival tree leaves yellow

The first line presents a human reality, and the second one juxtaposes by means of imaginative association to emphasize the aging of a human. That is, the hair turning gray is compared by the yellowed leaves for the visual effect. For haiku practice, one can dwell upon the images with a twist for these two versions:

SEVEN

> yearend
> more gray hair
> on his head

and

> autumn now
> leaves yellower
> and yellower

These two versions are used for discussion of reading classical Chinese poems with a haiku mind; these are not really good haiku. However, we need to know that this kind of writing practice is not unfamiliar to poets. Ezra Pound composed "Fan-Piece for Her Imperial Lord" which was adapted from Herbert Giles's translation of Ban Jieyu's (班婕妤, 48–6 BCE) poem titled "Song of the Round Fan" (团扇歌). He thought that Giles's translation was redundant and outdated in language and style, so he weeded out all the unnecessary parts in order to highlight the fan and its suggestion in a haiku format:

> O fan of white silk,
>   clear as frost on the grass-blade,
>   You also are laid aside. (Pound, *Personae* 108)

As a harbinger of Imagism, Pound was good at using images to express feelings. Therefore, instead of focusing on the concubine's feeling of abandonment, Pound chose the image of the silk fan. Not only the fan is also put aside, the frost and the blade may suggest cold, ill treatment and pain.

There are many more haiku-like couplets by other ancient Chinese poets. Here's one by Yu Liangshi (於良史) of the Tang dynasty:

> 掬水月在手
> 弄花香滿衣
>
> Scooping water and the moon is in the hands
> Viewing flowers and the fragrance stays on the dress

In Chinese literature, Yu, whose birth and death is unknown, has been well-known for this couplet about the interaction between human and nature. Both lines involve transference of senses either from touch to sight or from sight to smell that present a surprise, a delight, or a moment of interaction. For haiku practice, they can be rearranged as follows:

> scooping water
> the moon
> in my hands
>
> flower-viewing
> the dress covered
> with fragrance

The next two lines are from a quatrain by Meng Haoran (孟浩然, 689 – 740), a famous Chinese poet of the Tang dynasty:

> 野曠天低樹
> 江清月近人
>
> Far across wilderness trees touch the sky,
> In the clear water the moon is close to me.

This is the second couplet of Meng's quatrain. The first one is "Moor my boat by the misty isle, / my homesickness arrives at dusk," which describes the traveler's loneliness when homesickness grabs him. The second couplet focuses on the visual images, but the emotion hides behind images: the traveler looks afar with the thought of home, but his eyes meet only the distant trees and wilderness; he then looks down at the water moon; it is close but aloof. Loneliness becomes intense through looking far and near. With a haiku mind, one can reformat the two lines into haiku, as shown in these two:

> vast wilderness
> desolate trees
> against the sky

> clear water
> the moon
> close for a touch

Another example is a couplet from a wulü poem by Li Po (李白):

> 天清一雁遠
> 海闊孤帆遲

> In the clear sky a wild goose flies away
> On the vast sea a lone boat sails slowly

This couplet shows that classical Chinese poetry, in its essence, is concise in expressing human feelings through the images of nature. This use is a haiku element as well. These two lines express Li Po's feeling about seeing his friend off: even though his departure is like the wild goose flying away, his boat is reluctant to move fast. In a sense, images of a bird and a sail against the large perspectives of the sky and the sea add concrete meaning to inseparable friendship through a visual correspondence. These two lines can surely be used for haiku practice:

> clear sky
> a wild goose flies
> out of sight

> vast sea
> a lonely boat
> sails slowly

There are other couplets worth a mention. This one from a ten-line poem by Xie Tiao (謝朓, 464 – 499), a poet of the Southern dynasty:

> 魚戲新荷動
> 鳥散餘花落

Let me offer a word-by-word rendering in the haiku format:

> fish playing
> a new lotus leaf
> shaking
>
> birds dispersing
> last petals
> falling

Do they read like two haiku which show the observation of nature? Though the rendering is intentional with the use of the three-line pattern for the couplet, it is accurate in conveying the meaning of the original. Both have a cause-effect relationship that sets up a linkage for the visual correspondence.

The last couplet to be discussed for haiku practice is from a *wulü* verse by Wang Wei (王維, 692 – 761), a poet and painter of the Tang dynasty:

> 明月松間照
> 清泉石上流
>
> Bright moon shines through pines
> Clear spring flows over stones

Does this couplet provide a source for a haiku mind? Can it be condensed into one haiku? Does creative thinking challenge us to seek a visual correspondence between the moonlight and the spring water overflowing the stones? Here's a try:

> moonshine
> spring water flowing
> over stones

This example, together with all the couplets discussed, shows that reading with a haiku mind can be a good practice for creative thinking and haiku writing. Since my discussion centers on finding sources from classical Chinese poems as prompts for haiku writing, I give more attention to the couplets that read like haiku. Therefore, reading for an enlightening moment to stimulate haiku writing is necessary. The more one reads, and the better haiku one writes.

In fact, this writing process is evident in many poets, showing an influence or an image stored in memory. Bashō's haiku, "Rock azaleas, / flushed red / by cuckoo's cry" (74), surely embodies the influence of classical Chinese poetry. The historical records of the Shu State over two thousand years ago kept a tale that after renouncing his throne, the emperor transformed himself into a cuckoo. Each year when spring comes, he cried out blood that dyed azaleas red. The bleeding cry of the cuckoo became an allusion used frequently in classical Chinese poetry. Bashō's haiku seems to be especially inspired by this poetic line by Shu Yuexiang (舒岳祥, 1219–1298), a poet of the Song dynasty:

> 杜鵑啼血滴岩紅
>
> The cuckoo cries out blood, red drips on rocks

Here's another haiku of his that shows an echo of classical Chinese poetry:

> In the garden
> a sweaty shoe —
> scent of chrysanthemum. (Bashō 74)

Bashō's haiku echoes a poetic line of a classical Chinese poem by an anonymous poet:

> 踏花歸來馬蹄香
>
> Back from flower-viewing scent of horseshoes

These two haiku show that representation or rewriting from earlier literary sources was a haiku practice by Bashō when he wrote poems "in the so-called Chinese style" during the years of 1681-1684 (Shirane 19). It is a creative cross-pollination.

A reader familiar with Richard Wright's works may also realize that some of his haiku can be traced back to his novels or they show Wright's associative thinking when he composed haiku; that is, an image or a scene described in his fiction would appear in his haiku mind. For example, Wright wrote several street-sweeping haiku which might come from his own street-sweeping experience mentioned in *Black Boy*. Here's one of them: "Wisps of winter fog / Left by the streetsweeper's broom / Along the gutters" (120).

Ian Marshall is another haiku practitioner who turned to Henry David Thoreau's Walden to look for sources for haiku writing. His *Walden by Haiku* shows an intriguing haiku experiment. He extracted three hundred haiku from Thoreau's *Walden*. For example, from Thoreau's paragraph—"The soil, it appears, is suited to the seed, for it has sent its radical downward, and it may now send its shoot upward also with confidence. Why has man rooted himself thus firmly in the earth, but that he may rise in the same proportion into the heavens above?"—Marshall found this haiku: "a seed / rooted firmly in the earth / rising to the heavens." He also provided a note of the process of creating this haiku: "In the haiku version of this, I've left out the metaphoric reference to 'man' as the seed in question, but perhaps that metaphoric dimension comes across with the reference to the 'heavens,' which suggests spiritual as well as botanical yearning" (104). Marshall's practice shows a creative haiku mind in finding the sources for haiku writing. This is a creative process of reimagining, reproducing, and representing Thoreau's mind as well.

When I read Eudora Welty's *Delta Wedding*, I realized her novel could be a mine of haiku sources and gleaned one hundred haiku from it for my chapbook *Found Haiku* from Eudora Welty's *Delta Wedding*. For example, in a paragraph about Laura's ride to the delta, Welty presents this vivid description of an observation, "In the passenger car every window was propped open with a stick of kindling wood. A breeze blew through, hot and then cool, fragrant of the woods and yellow flowers and of the train. The yellow butterflies flew in at any window, out at any other, and outdoors one of them could keep up with the train, which then seemed to be racing with a butterfly" (2). Seeing a haiku moment in this description, I selected the images of breeze, yellow butterfly, and window and juxtaposed them in this found haiku:

> delta breeze
> a yellow butterfly
> through the window (4)

To conclude, my discussion shows a way of reading, a way of thinking, and a way of writing "found haiku." It can be used as a way of teaching in a creative writing class. This reading and writing practice requires the reader to examine the sources closely and select the images suitable for a haiku. It is also an intriguing experiment that inspires and enriches a haiku mind.

Works Cited

Bashō, Matsuo. *On Love and Barley: Haiku of Bashō.* Trans and intro. Lucien Stryk. Penguin, 1985.

Henderson, Harold G. *An Introduction to Haiku.* Doubleday, 1958.

Marshall, Ian. *Walden by Haiku.* U of Georgia P, 2009.

Pound, Ezra. Personae: *The Collected Poems of Ezra Pound.* New Directions, 1926.

Shirane, Haruo. *Traces of Dreams: Landscape, Cultural Memory, and the Poetry of Bashō.* Stanford UP, 1998.

Welty, Eudora. *Delta Wedding.* Harcourt, 1946.

Wright, Richard. *Haiku: This Other World.* Arcade Publishing, 1998.

Zheng, JQ. *Found Haiku from Eudora Welty's Delta Wedding.* Yazoo River P, 2006. (https://www.thehaikufoundation.org/omeka/items/show/1539).

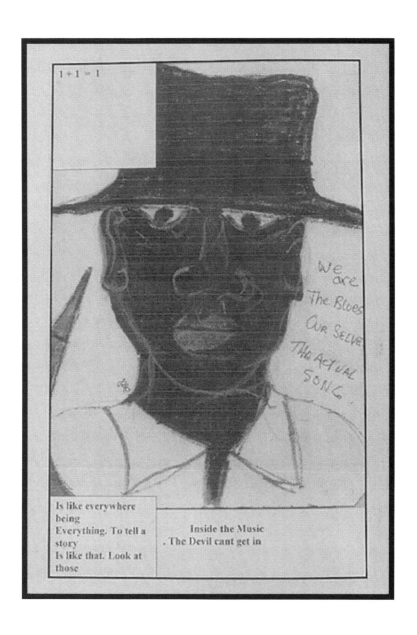

Poet/Artist: Amiri Baraka

Recent Dissertations and Theses on Haiku (and Senryū, Renga, and Tanka) in English

Josh Hockensmith

ABSTRACT: In *JUXTA* 2.1, Randy Brooks presented an annotated bibliography of graduate theses and dissertations published between 1950-2014 about haiku, senryu, renga, and tanka. Below is an addendum to that bibliography, listing subsequently published papers as well as some earlier ones that were not included in Brooks's bibliography. Where appropriate, I've used the same categories and sub-categories that Brooks used in organizing his bibliography. I've added or revised category headings for papers that didn't fit into an existing one.
All information is gathered from the ProQuest Dissertations and Theses database. All quotations are from the papers' abstracts. The papers may be available to you through the interlibrary loan service at your local library, or through the ProQuest database itself if you have access to an academic institution that subscribes to it.
By no means is this a comprehensive list – each new search executed with a slight variation on terms or search conditions turns up new titles, and other papers on the subject surely exist in addition to those indexed in the ProQuest database.

Theses on American Haiku Poets

Monteleone, Amanda. "Gerald Vizenor's Transcultural Haiku Dreamscape."[1] The University of Texas at Arlington, 2018. MA Thesis. 82 pages.

> "While many of Vizenor's haiku speak to Native American tribal values, a strictly Native American reading stifles other cultural qualities present in his haiku dreamscape. My analysis of Vizenor's haiku in Japanese literary and cultural contexts provides insights into how his poetry specifically relates to a Japanese literary tradition as well as a Native American tradition, opening doors of further inquiry and analysis toward Vizenor's writings outside of Native American studies."

Theses on American Poetry and Haiku[2]

Arimitsu, Michio. "Black Notes on Asia: Composite Figurations of Asia in the African American Transcultural Imagination, 1923-2013." Harvard University, 2014. Dissertation. 305 pages.

> "In order to understand the full complexity and heterogeneity of the African American imagination from the beginning of the twentieth century to the present, it is necessary to account for cultural ebbs and flows, echoes and reverberations, beyond the United States, Europe and Africa, to include Asia. Rediscovering the hitherto overlooked traces and reflections of Asia within

---

1. An essay, "Living in Community: The More-than-Human World in Gerald Vizenor's Haiku," by the author and adapted from this thesis, is published elsewhere in this issue of *JUXTA*.
2. I decided against using subcategories such as Modern American Poets and The Beats here as Dr. Brooks did, because the examples presented tend to straddle or expand beyond those categories, and because there are few enough titles listed that they are easily browsable. Looking ahead, perhaps a cumulative version of this bibliography could be adapted to a format that incorporates hyperlinked tags, so that a title could be tagged "The Beats" and "The Black Arts Movement," for example, for easy cross-discipline access to researchers approaching from different angles of interest.

> the African American imagination, this dissertation argues that Asia has provided numerous African American authors and intellectuals, canonized as well as forgotten, with additional or alternative cultural resources that liberated them from, or at least helped them destabilize, what they considered as the constraining racial and nationalist discourse of the United States."

Gilbert, Matthew. "Fir-Flower Petals on a Wet, Black Bough: Constructing New Poetry through Asian Aesthetics in Early Modernist Poets." East Tennessee State University, 2019. MA Thesis. 54 pages.

Kim, Heejung. "The Other American Poetry and Modernist Poetics: Richard Wright, Jack Kerouac, Sonia Sanchez, James Emanuel, and Lenard Moore." Kent State University, 2018. Dissertation. 220 pages.

> "This dissertation explores each poet's haiku and investigates whether it is just an escape from the traditional style of American poetry or if the American haiku is truly a different poetic genre with its own distinct identity. This study examines each poet's characteristics, as well as his or her limitations as a haiku poet."

Tate, Bronwen Rose. "'Putting it All Down, Leaving it All Out': Scale in Post-1945 American Poetry." Stanford University, 2014. Dissertation. 316 pages.

> "I analyze extremes of poetic brevity and length as complementary, distinctly postmodern responses to the increasing marginalization of poetry in the period following World War II… In a chapter on the post-1945 haiku boom, for example, I demonstrate how poets embraced the Japanese form as a refreshing alternative to lyric inwardness. In my readings of poems by Niedecker, Jack Kerouac, and others, I theorize the divergent responses to haiku as acts of adoption, inclusion, or adaptation."

SEVEN

Theses on Japanese Haiku and Related Literature

Crowson, Michelle Kyoko. "Proposing a Poetics of Opposition in the Haikai of Kobayashi Issa." University of Utah, 2012. MA Thesis. 82 pages.

—. "Before the World: Kaga No Chiyo & the Rustic-Feminine Margins of Japanese Haiku." University of Oregon, 2020. Dissertation. 201 pages.

> "This dissertation tracks the transformation of the merchant-class female poet, Kaga no Chiyo, from a minor supplementary position as a collected feminine object to an interlocutor and exemplar of post-Bashō poetics in regional circulation. I argue that discourses on the fall of *haikai* poetry among eighteenth-century male practitioners, combined with the rise of an eccentric *bunjin* "literati") consciousness, led to a pattern of rural male poets collecting women as casual supplements to masculine-coded poetic communities, part of a larger valorization of a poetics of simplicity and lightness."

Malissa, Samuel Asher. "Made in Translation: Japanese Translators & Japanese Literature in English, 1880-1945." Yale University, 2018. Dissertation. 194 pages.

> "This study of the proactive introduction of Japanese language texts into English by Japanese people, termed "push translation," addresses a gap in translation historiography, which has largely overlooked this practice in favor of translations into Japanese or translations out of Japanese by Westerners."

Mewhinney, Matthew Stanhope. "The Lyric Forms of the Literati Mind: Yosa Buson, Ema Saikō, Masaoka Shiki and Natsume Sōseki." University of California, Berkeley, 2018. Dissertation. 213 pages.

> "The dissertation shows what the lyric writings of Buson, Saikō, Shiki, and Sōseki can tell us about lyric thinking, subjectivity, and the philosophy of poetic form."

Xie, Kai. "Remapping the Sino-Japanese Dialectic: Sino-Japanese Interplay in Linked Verse Compositions of Japan, 14th to 17th Centuries." University of Washington, 2017. Dissertation. 240 pages.

> "This dissertation examines the juxtaposition, interaction, and integration of what Japanese authors conceived of as "Japanese" and "Chinese" elements in linked verse compositions of Japan from the 14th to 17th centuries… This dissertation also studies Japanese linked verse that heavily engaged with Chinese elements, focusing on compositions by the circle of Matsuo Bashō, the best-known poet in early modern Japan. On the one hand, I explore various ways Bashō' circle appropriated Chinese literature in the "Chinese style" popular linked verse, demonstrating that their absorption of Chinese literature and thought on the spiritual level contributed to sublimating popular linked verse into a serious art. On the other hand, this dissertation seeks to demonstrate that Bashō's reception of Chinese texts was sometimes mediated by Yamaguchi Sodō, who had profound knowledge in Chinese studies and was also a respected poet of popular linked verse."

Theses on Haiku and Linguistics

Burton, Benjamin Robert. "Playing Japanese: Fostering Semantic Language Play in a Japanese as a Foreign Language Classroom." University of Washington, 2020. Master of Japanese Linguistics Thesis. 98 pages.

> "The study shows how playful language learning tasks can encourage creativity, participation, and expression within the language classroom. I conclude by arguing for more serious consideration of play as not only a driver of linguistic development but also an essential aspect of language learning."

SEVEN

Theses on Using Haiku in Other Academic Disciplines

Magge, Arjun. "Fixed Verse Generation using Neural Word Embeddings." Arizona State University, 2016. MS Thesis. 94 pages.

> "This thesis presents a novel approach to fixed verse poetry generation using neural word embeddings ... The verses generated by the system are evaluated using rhyme, rhythm, syllable counts and stress patterns. These computational features of language are considered for generating haikus, limericks and iambic pentameter verses. The generated poems are evaluated using a Turing test on both experts and non-experts ... Although the system does not pass the Turing test, the results from the Turing test suggest an improvement of over 17% when compared to previous methods which use Turing tests to evaluate poetry generators."

Creative Writing Theses with Haiku and Related Literature[3]

Brunson, David. 2021. "Fault Lines: Poems and Translations. University of Arkansas, 2021. MFA Thesis. 130 pages.

Dally, Andrew. "Medium Extra Value." The University of Mississippi, 2018. MFA Thesis. 60 pages.

Heron, Claudia M. "Considerable Things." Mills College, 2012. MFA Thesis. 87 pages.

Hosek, Cody Donovan. "Might Could." University of South Carolina, 2020. MFA Thesis. 60 pages.

---

3. I've limited the selections here to thesis manuscripts in which haiku or related forms are mentioned as the primary mode of composition. It's worth noting that a much larger number of search results showed students using haiku as one among many other forms in their manuscripts, indicating that haiku-related formats have attained a somewhat equal footing with traditionally Western forms in academic creative writing practice.

Lucky, Robert Wayne. The Armchair Daoist. University of Texas at El Paso, 2012. MFA Thesis. 80 pages.

Theses in English on Haiku in Other Non-Japanese Languages

Sciarra-Laos, Emilia. "Experimental Poetry in Four Authors: Tablada, De Campos, Padín and Brossa." State University of New York at Albany, 2013. Dissertation. 189 pages.

Haiku and Music Composition[4]

Barnsfather, Samantha Ryan. "Nationalism and Eclecticism in the Selected Songs of Ronald Stevenson (b.1928)." University of Florida, 2013. Dissertation. 151 pages.

Chang, Yu-Hsin. "An Analysis of Toshio Hosokawa: Lotus Under the Moonlight for Piano and Orchestra." University of California, Davis, 2018. Dissertation. 62 pages.

> "The second chapter draws on reference to haiku written by Matsuo Bashō (1644-1694) to explain the ideas of stasis in Lotus. The third chapter dives into showing the influence of "nothingness," a philosophical concept at the aesthetic root of silence/sound polarity."

Finkel, Joseph. "Negotiating Music and Politics: John Cage's United States Bicentennial Compositions "Lecture on the Weather" and "Renga with Apartment House 1776". Arizona State University, 2015. Dissertation. [# of pages N/A.]

4. In Dr. Brooks's earlier bibliography, papers on this topic were included under the category "Theses on Using Haiku in Other Academic Disciplines." I encountered enough results that it seemed worthwhile to break them out under their own category heading. The subject of how haiku principles inform composition in another medium (music) — and how those principles have translated to and evolved within another Western creative practice — may be of great interest to haiku poets.

Jin, Jing. "Portfolio of Compositions with Technical Commentary." University of London, King's College (United Kingdom), 2017. Dissertation. [# of pages N/A.]

Lewis, Kevin D. ""The Miracle of Unintelligibility": The Music and Invented Instruments of Lucia Dlugoszewski." University of Cincinnati, 2011. Dissertation. 105 pages.

Mabary, Sarah Hogrefe. "A Performer's Guide to Six Song Cycles Composed between 1959 and 2010 by Mississippi Composers." The University of Southern Mississippi, 2012. Dissertation. 107 pages.

Morgan, Jennifer. "Violin Haiku: Text/music Relationship, Program and Structure." The Florida State University, 2014. Dissertation. 102 pages.

> "Four pieces by American composers that feature the violin and include the word haiku in their titles provide a thought-provoking forum in which to examine the nature and degrees of text-prominence within a non-vocal work and the possible transfers of haiku poetic form to music. The pieces discussed are *12 Haiku for Speaking Voice and Violin* by John Holland, *Suite: Eight Haiku by Richard Wright* by Judah Adashi, "Spring" from *Haiku for Solo Strings* by Benjamin Whiting, and "Haiku" from *Duet for Violin and Harpsichord*, Op. 122 by Alan Hovhaness."

Oliver, Desmond Mark. "Cultural Appropriation in Messiaen's Rhythmic Language." University of Oxford (United Kingdom), 2016. Dissertation. [# of pages N/A.]

"Chapter 4 contextualises Messiaen's Japanese poem Sept haïkaï (1962) in relation to other European Orientalist artworks of the late-nineteenth and early-twentieth centuries, and also in relation to Michael Sullivan's (1987: 209) three-tiered definitions of japonism."

Otter, Franner. "Composition Portfolio." University of Salford (United Kingdom), 2011. Dissertation. [# of pages N/A.]

Roberts, Lillian Channelle. "Image, Narrative, and Concept of Time in Valerie Capers' Song Cycle "Song of the Seasons"." University of Nevada, Las Vegas, 2016. Dissertation. 143 pages.

> "Primarily known as a renowned jazz pianist, Valerie Capers is a blind, African-American woman composer who defied all odds by becoming the first blind graduate of The Juilliard School . . . According to Capers, *Song of the Seasons* is "a celebration of life" and was inspired by Japanese haiku, a Japanese poetic form that illuminates the human condition through imagistic themes of nature, love, and death. The cycle of revolving seasons is connected through figurative language of the composer's own text, European art song, opera, and African-American Jazz."

Shin, Dong Jin. "Beyond Orientalism: Reconsidering East Asian Influence in Early Twentieth-Century European Music." University of Florida, 2020. Dissertation. 188 pages.

> "This dissertation problematizes the application of Edward Said's concept of Orientalism in researching East Asian influence in Western art music and reassesses the instrumental receptions and representations of East Asia in Western music. It argues that, by taking Said's concept Orientalism as a self-reflexive tool, Western scholars have taken a privileged position in judging the Other's victimhood and benefitted their scholarly position in US-centric academia. Many studies on cross-cultural influences criticize the cultural appropriations and derogative representations of East Asia in Western music based on the premise of power imbalance between two cultural areas. This study focuses, however, on the positive impact of East Asian culture in early twentieth-century French music by means of "Japonisme.""

Sloan, Steven. "The Seasons: 30 Haiku for Flute, Clarinet, Violin, Cello, Mezzo-Soprano, and Baritone." Bowling Green State University, 2017. Master of Music Thesis. 86 pages.

"*The Seasons* is a 30-movement work for mezzo-soprano, baritone, and Pierrot ensemble (flute, clarinet in b-flat, violin, violoncello, and piano). The text for the work consists of 30 haiku written by the composer — seven haiku for each of the four seasons, plus a pair of transitional poems between summer and autumn, then autumn and winter. There are seven songs in each season — a nod to the father of the Pierrot ensemble, Arnold Schönberg, and his love of numerology. The seasons slowly infect each other as they progress, paying tribute to their natural evolution."

Stankis, Jessica Elizabeth. "Maurice Ravel as Miniaturist through the Lens of *Japonisme*." University of California, Santa Barbara, 2012. Dissertation. 292 pages.

Walshaw, Trevor Stansfield. "Roberto Gerhard: Explorer and Synthesist." University of Huddersfield (United Kingdom), 2013. Dissertation. [# of pages N/A.]

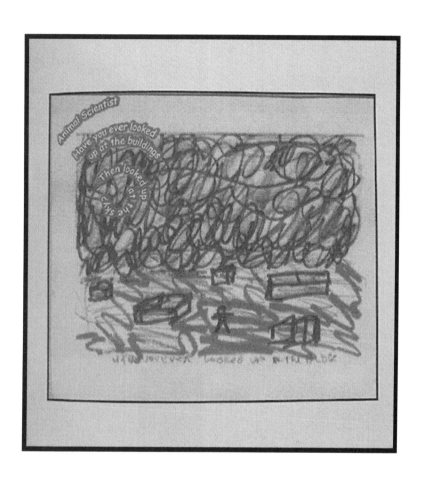

Poet/Artist: Amiri Baraka

The Pleasures and Heartbreaks of the Road:

A Review of *Matsuo Bashō: Travel Writings.*

ADAM L. KERN

> Carter, Steven D. *Matsuo Bashō: Travel Writings*. Boston, MA: Hackett Publishing Company, 2020. 304 pages, hard cover and paperback. ISBN 978-1624668579.

Steven D. Carter, Yamato Ichihashi Chair in Japanese History and Civilization, emeritus, Stanford University, has written authoritatively on Japanese poetry for decades. His *Traditional Japanese Poetry: An Anthology* (Stanford, 1993) and *Haiku Before Haiku: From the Renga Masters to Bashō* (Columbia, 2011) in particular are required reading in many college courses on the subject. As might be expected, then, Carter's latest, *Matsuo Bashō: Travel Writings*, as the culmination of a distinguished career, is top-notch.

The work presents all six of Matsuo Bashō's (1644–1694) literary travel writings, a combination of graceful prose (haibun) with what today is called haiku, though there are also 14-syllabet "short verses" (*tanku*) as well. Carter arranges these half dozen writings in chronological order by date of journey, more or less (since some works drew from more than one journey), rather than by date of composition, let alone of publication (since all six works were published posthumously if not titled retrospectively). To wit: *Bones Bleaching in the Fields* (*Nozarashi kikō*, published 1698), was based on Bashō's trip of 1684; *A Pilgrimage to Kashima* (*Kashima mōde*, 1752), 1687; *Knapsack Notes* (*Oi no kobumi*, 1709), 1687-1688; *A Journey to Sarashina* (*Sarashina kikō*, 1704), 1689; *The Narrow Road through the Hinterlands* (*Oku no hosomichi*, 1702), 1689; and *The Saga Diary* (*Saga nikki*, 1753), 1691.

In addition to the translations, *Travel Writings* contains a fine introduction, a glossary of literary terms, indices, and appendices consisting of several brief essays: "Travel in Bashō's Day," "*Haikai* Poetry in Bashō's Day," "Bashō and Religion," "Bashō's Family and Other Relationships," "The Questions of Genre and Titles," "Fact and/or Fiction: The Challenge of Sora's Diary," "Excerpts from Linked-Verse Sequences," "Figures of Importance in the Texts," and "Places of Importance in the Text." These essays help contextualize the various travel writings succinctly.

To the extent that there is a major argument, it has to do with situating Bashō as a wayfaring poet whose interest in the hybrid genre of *haibun* travel writing was more spiritual-artistic than punctiliously journalistic—let alone devoutly "religious," in the sense of following one religion to the exclusion of others; for Bashō drew deeply from the wells of the major religious, philosophical, ideological, and cultural systems of thought, rather than being committed to Zen Buddhism to the exclusion of Confucianism, Shinto, Daoism, and so on.

Of course, this is hardly the first time Bashō's literary travel writings have been translated and discussed as a whole in English. David Barnhill did as much in *Bashō's Journey: The Literary Prose of Matsuo Bashō* (SUNY, 2005). So, too, did Donald Keene before him in *Travelers of a Hundred Ages* (Columbia, 1989). Keene took up not only all six "travel diaries" (as he calls them), but also many of the other major Japanese literary diaries over the past millennium, thereby situating Bashō's literary travel writings in broad comparative context. Yet by focusing exclusively on Bashō's writings, Carter is admirably able to delve into greater depth. The way Carter does this uniformly across all six works, not just Bashō's *chef d'oeuvre* among them, is perhaps the main contribution of *Travel Writings*.

When it comes to *Oku no hosomichi* itself, Carter presents related information, such as some original *renga* sequences, thereby augmenting our understanding. For this reader, at least, such extensive treatment makes for a richer, more satisfying encounter with Bashō's works in translation. Although Keene's versions have a distinctive voice that makes them a pleasure to read, Carter's translations are more accurate without sacrificing overall readability. If Keene too often lets his style overwhelm the meaning, Carter rarely lets the meaning overwhelm his style.

Keene's term "travel diary" inadvertently suggests that Bashō was a faithful chronicler of his lived experiences on the road. This he most certainly was not. After all, as is well known, Bashō exerted poetic license with more than the poetry in *Oku no hosomichi*—which Carter describes as "the most complete and carefully written of Bashō's travel writings" (249). This license is indisputable, especially after the comparatively more factual account of Bashō's journey, as described by the man's traveling companion Kawai Sora (1649–1710) in *Sora tabi nikki* (*Sora's Travel Diary*), came to light in 1943. Carter's titular and central term "travel writings," by contrast, admits the possibility of literary fashioning, which Carter pinpoints as distinguishing Bashō's travel writings. The main strength of *Travel Writings*, in my opinion, stems from how this deliberate literary fashioning is drawn out and celebrated by a scholar-translator at the top of his game.

Oku no hosomichi, it should be noted, has been translated at least a dozen times into English. Maybe more. Carter's translation therefore might be considered against the major efforts by David Barnhill, Dorothy Britton, Cid Corman and Kamaike Susumu, Sam Hamill, Donald Keene, Helen Craig McCullough, Earl Miner, Yuasa Nobuyuki, Hiroaki Sato, and especially Haruo Shirane, among others. Of these, the translations by Carter and Shirane are the most unfailingly accurate. Yet Carter's translation is also eminently readable. Thus, if assigning a single book in an undergraduate course on Bashō or haiku or *Oku no hosomichi*, I would choose Carter over Noboyuki (Penguin, 1966) and Barnhill, though depending on availability, I might also opt for Shirane or Hamill.

In addition to readability, Carter's prose translations are first rate: clear, reliable, accurate, with little if any room for stylistic improvement. By way of example, here's Carter's rendition of the celebrated opening passage to *Oku no hosomichi*. To my ear, Carter's tone and cadence pretty much match those of Bashō's original:

> The moon, the sun — these are wayfarers down the generations; so too the years are travelers that come and go. For those who bob their lives away on boats or lead horses as old age approaches, travel is daily life, travel is home. Many among the ancients died on the road, and I, too, for some years past had felt the tug of winds that tatter the clouds, unable to put rambling from my mind. So it was that after a jaunt on ocean shores, I cleared the cobwebs from my broken-down hut last autumn, and as the year drew to a close set my heart on making for Shirakawa Barrier as soon as the skies turned hazy with spring. Lured by the god of wanderlust, I could not keep my mind on anything; beckoned by the god of the road, I could not hold my hand to any task. After mending the holes in my trousers, putting a new cord on my rain hat, and bracing my kneecaps with moxa treatments, I was thinking of the moon at Matsushima and feeling restless (97-98).

SEVEN

Likewise, Carter's translations of the poems are themselves poetry, with some gems and few if any let-downs. Here are two of my favorites from *Knapsack Notes*:

> A deer's horns—
> just starting to show themselves
> as we part.
>
> *shika no tsuno / mazu hitofushi no / wakare kana*
>
> Ah, the many things
> they call back to mind:
> cherry blossoms.
>
> *samazama no / koto omidasu / sakura kana*

And a brief sampling from *Narrow Road through the Hinterlands*:

> The fleas, the lice —
> and a horse pissing
> by my pillow.
>
> *nomi shirami / uma no bari suru / makuramoto*

This version captures the sense of complaint better than any other.

And here's one that does justice to a celebrated verse, even though some translators might have been tempted to modify "cicada's drone" with a pronoun in a misguided effort to avoid Tontoism (Paul O. Williams's coinage for the unfortunate dropping of grammatical articles inadvertently suggesting, when it comes to haiku, a kind of Orientalist stereotyping of non-native speakers of English trying to speak English but failing):

> Such stillness!
> The very rocks are pierced
> by cicada's drone.
>
> *shizukasa ya / iwa ni shimiiru / semi no koe*

Interestingly, Carter deploys full stops and the pronoun "it" in his translations more than just about any other major translator:

> My grass hut, too,
> now home to someone else.
> A doll's house.
>
> *kusa no to mo / sumikawarau yo zo / hina no ie*
>
> In the same house
> pleasure women sleeping, too.
> Bush clover and the moon.
>
> *hitotsuie ni / yūjo mo netari / hagi to tsuki*
>
> Over rough seas
> it stretches off to Sado —
> the River of Heaven.
>
> *araumi ya / sado ni yokotau / amanogawa*

The "it" here feels warranted for focusing attention on the majestic final phrase.

> It takes the hot sun
> and pushes it into the sea —
> Mogami River.
>
> *atsuki hi o / umi ni iretaru / mogamigawa*

The momentary confusion between the double occurrence of "it" here, however, which is easily enough resolved, replicates the suspension of meaning until the very last word of the original as well. Still, some readers may wonder if such repetition is really warranted.

This is an exceedingly minor grumble. One which in no way impugns the excellence of *Travel Writings*, especially given the quality of its scholarship; for Carter has engaged deeply and meaningfully with all of the major Japanese scholarly sources, including recent ones, which is to say the annotated editions of the sometimes multiple manuscripts of Bashō's literary travel writings in their original editions. And while of course conversant with the germane English-language scholarship and translations, to his credit Carter is by no means unduly swayed by or beholden to those works. With the possible exception of Shirane, Carter's scholarship is unrivalled, synthesizing multiple Japanese source texts and annotated scholarly works into an organic whole. If anything, the footnoted annotations are so fine grained, they may well be more appropriate to a scholarly audience or even just specialists than a general readership.

The result is a literary translation that does justice to the original, making one feel every bit as dusty, road weary, and breathless as Bashō himself, as narrator-protagonist, comes across in the original texts. Destined to delight readers with its vibrant, spot-on translations, this definitive collection of haiku grandmaster Bashō's travel writings, in prose as well as poetry, conveys the exquisite pleasures and heartbreaks of the road as a metaphor for life itself. At the end of the day, Steven Carter's *Matsuo Bashō: Travel Writings* should probably be counted as the best English-language study of its subject to date, unlikely to be eclipsed anytime soon.

Appreciation and Appropriation:

A Review of *American Haiku: New Readings*

J. Zimmerman

> Toru Kiuchi, Editor. *American Haiku: New Readings* (2018). Lanham, MD: Lexington Books. Hardcover, 356 pages. ISBN 978-1-4985-2717-0.

American Haiku: New Readings (2018), edited by haiku poet Toru Kiuchi, former professor of English at Nihon University, presents 14 chapters (3 by himself, 3 by Yoshinobu Hakutani, and 8 by different authors) on haiku development in the United States. Despite the subtitle of "New Readings," Kiuchi acknowledges 5 of the chapters as previously published between 2007 and 2011; additionally, I discovered Chapters 2 and 9 are primarily republications from a 2009 book.

The first part of the book presents five chapters on aspects in the history of American haiku. The second part offers nine chapters of criticism of haiku and haiku-like poems by poets influenced by diverse cultures and with different personalities and interests. Two-thirds of the second half's chapters concern work of African

American writers, editor Kiuchi claiming in his Introduction that, "The new trend in American haiku is African American haiku aesthetic" (xiii).

What would have enriched the collection for me would have been at least one chapter that analyzed the relationship of American haiku to Western poetry trends, such as Modernism, Postmodernism, New Formalism, and performance poetry. Given the times and the material, another welcome addition would have been a chapter on cultural appreciation versus cultural appropriation.

Kiuchi opens Part I, "History," with his "Yone Noguchi's Invention of English-Language Haiku" (Chapter 1): "Not only did Noguchi play an important role in the translation of haiku; he is also the inventor as well as disseminator of English-language haiku." (4) Kiuchi quotes seven of Noguchi's haiku as plausibly the first haiku created in English. Written in 1897, the haiku were published that same year in Noguchi's collection *Seen & Unseen* that he distributed to many poets including Ezra Pound. Initially, Noguchi followed a 5-7-5-syllable pattern in English; later he advocated for shorter haiku.

Yoshinobu Hakutani's "Ezra Pound, Imagism, and Haiku" (Chapter 2) attributes Pound's awareness of *hokku* to Noguchi, emphasizes Pound's view of the image as dynamic rather than static, and notes Pound's call for directness and clarity of expression. The chapter is very similar to one in Hakutani's *Haiku and Modernist Poetics* (2009).

Toshio Kimura's brief (8-page) section is possibly my favorite: "Mutual Influence between the American and the Japanese Haiku: The History of American Haiku" (Chapter 3). Kimura reminds us that: "Shiki [Masaoka (1867–1902)] separated hokku from the other following lines [in linked verse] and made it new as the new haiku form . . . composed by one poet . . . [in] the Western manner" (59). In addition:

> *Shasei* (Sketching) that Shiki advocated as a new method for haiku seemed to be influenced by the Western realism of the 19th century ... The birth of haiku itself could be said to be brought about by the American influence through Japan's opening up and modernization. (59)

Jim Kacian's "100 Years of Haiku in the United States: An Overview" (Chapter 4) serves in particular as a useful commentary on *Haiku in English: the First Hundred Years*, the 2013 anthology he co-edited with Philip Rowland and Allan Burns, and from which he selected a predominant portion of this chapter's haiku. Kacian credits W. G. Aston as the first to publish haiku in English, in his 1877 book of Japanese grammar, though the text does not document whether the three anonymously quoted "hokku" (66) were originals or translations; given the context, I opine that it is likely they translated poems by others.[1]

In "Haiku in Higher Education" (Chapter 5) Randy Brooks recaps and expands on his previous bibliographies (of articles and theses) published in *Juxta* and *Modern Haiku*. He concludes with a walk-through of his Millikin University course "Global Haiku Traditions."

Part II, "Criticism," begins with Hakutani's "Richard Wright's Haiku, Zen, and the African 'Primal Outlook on Life' " (Chapter 6). Hakutani shows Wright (1908–60) to have studied and been influenced by the haiku of poets from seventeenth and eighteenth century Japan, and to have blended aspects of an "African worldview that human beings are not at the center of the universe, a worldview that corresponds with that of Zen." (170-171) This chapter was published previously.

---

1. Sappho is the classic example of a poet (one of many) quoted by grammarians. Academician Anne Carson in her luminous *If Not, Winter: Fragments of Sappho* (2002) tells us about: "the bits of Sappho cited by ancient scholiasts, grammarians, metricians, etc., who want a dab of poetry to document some proposition of their own" (xi).

In "Zen Buddhism in Richard Wright's Haiku" (Chapter 7), editor Kiuchi quotes Blyth's list of "thirteen characteristics of the Zen state of mind which the creation and appreciation of haiku demand: selflessness, loneliness, grateful acceptance, . . ." (182) and then quotes some of Wright's haiku infused with those qualities. This chapter was published previously.

With "African American Haiku and Aesthetic Attitude" (Chapter 8), John Zheng "hopes that readers, researchers, as well as poets will appreciate with new eyes African American haiku and aesthetic attitude" (202). Many poets whose poems Zheng discusses use the haiku in sequences to form longer poems. Zheng begins with "African American haiku" from the 1920s and quotes Lewis G. Alexander that its "real value is not in its physical directness but in its psychological indirectness" (194). Zheng quotes short haiku-like poems by Langston Hughes. He offers Robert Hayden's insight that a haiku is "a small arc for which the reader supplies the rest of circle (sic)" (195), which nicely expresses the point of haiku being suggestive. Thirty-three other African American poets are acknowledged, Zheng writing, "some are crafted haikuists, and some may be . . . tourists in the haiku land" (201). This chapter was published previously.

In "Jack Kerouac's Haiku and The Dharma Bums" (Chapter 9), Hakutani describes Kerouac (1922-69) as "going around the country as a Buddhist bum . . . traveling as if he were a roaming bard like Bashō" (215). Kerouac proposed and wrote the "Western Haiku" as a "kind of haiku" being a "sentence that's short and sweet with a sudden jump of thought" (218). In effect this chapter is previously published, being heavily derived from Hakutani's *Haiku and Modernist Poetics* (2009).

With "Sonia Sanchez's *Morning Haiku* and the Blues" (Chapter 10), Heejung Kim (a Ph.D. candidate at the time) explores how Sanchez "conflated the aesthetic principles underlying classical

SEVEN

haiku, such as *yugen*, *sabi*, and *wabi*, with those of the blues" (229). Kim reports that instead of "lamenting the tragic history of black people, she [Sanchez] is striving to find the unity and reconciliation of the races" (237).

In "Those 'Negro slaves, dark purple ripened plums'..." (Chapter 11), Virginia Whaley Smith compares Jean Toomer's 1923 "experimental novel *Cane* that launched[2] the Harlem Renaissance Movement" (243) with African American poet James A. Emanuel's "1999 collection *Jazz from the Haiku King* . . . [which] parodies Toomer's subject matter concerning the degradation and dehumanization of 'Negro slaves' and free persons scripted in *Cane*" (244). This chapter is abruptly different in style from the rest of the book, introducing phrasing and vocabulary of college classrooms, such as:

> Emanuel's . . . *Jazz from the Haiku King* . . . because of Toomer's microtextual jazz theme, magnifies and temporarily and spatially upgrades narratives about Black Atlantic (African/African American) captives by creating jazzed haiku poetry as his medium of international messaging. (244)

Smith states that in *Cane*, "The blues song in haiku format . . . starts the action" (245), but I would have liked a more convincing quotation. She does quote Toomer's "five- and four-line haiku stanzas" (246) but to me those are end-rhymed quatrains and cinquains (typically rhymed abbaa) in iambics and tending to pentameter. By contrast, Smith quotes haiku-like (or at least 5-7-5 syllabic) poems by Emanuel, the first being his "keystone poem [titled] 'The Haiku King' " (245): "Haiku king subject / royal; seventeen each meal / serve him. Food royal" (245). Smith notes that Emanuel created "an eclectic, postmodernist jazz haiku

---

2. However, Wikipedia reports that Toomer was "commonly associated with the Harlem Renaissance, though he actively resisted the association" (retrieved July 30, 2021, from https://en.wikipedia.org/wiki/Jean_Toomer).

narrative of redemption, regeneration, and healing" (273) while discarding many haiku traditions as in his 1993 long poem "The Middle Passage Blues":

> Emanuel has broken all of Bashō's tight rules, and has resorted to a seven-line, nineteen-line, seven-line, and ten-line cluster of four stanzas that make the long poem to appear like a truncated, 13th-century renga or series of linked verses . . . [of] over one hundred individual haiku that have been clustered by section title. (259)

In my experience it is Bashō's interpreters rather than Bashō who have asserted "tight rules." Furthermore, I would have liked the book, especially in this chapter, to discuss how far the haiku form can be adapted and "all" the "tight rules" broken before a resulting poem is appropriating the name "haiku" but should be called something else. A version of this chapter was published previously.

Kiuchi returns with: "Creating African American Haiku Form: Lenard D. Moore's Poetic Artistry" (Chapter 12). Moore (1958 –) began reading Japanese haiku in translation in 1982. He was soon writing his own nature-imbued haiku that had a relaxed resonance with the Japanese tradition of foregrounding nature. Concurrently he reclaimed aspects such as self-ownership of the body that had been stolen from African Americans during years of slavery:

> a black woman
> breastfeeding her infant —
> the autumn moon (281)

In the 1990's Moore began to explore other forms that included the one-line haiku, the renku in collaboration, and haiku sequences such as *Desert Storm: A Brief History*. The article could have been enriched for this collection by adding Moore's continued haiku development in the quarter century since 1995. This chapter was previously published.

Ce Rosenow presents "Cid Corman and Haiku: The Poetics of 'Livingdying'" (Chapter 13), centering on a "livingdying philosophy" and the belief by Corman (1924 – 2004) "that in each moment humans are simultaneously living and dying" (287). Rosenow shows Corman's adaptation of the haiku form (such as by using titles and line enjambment and by writing multiverse poems especially with a 2-3-2 or a 3-3-3 syllable pattern for each stanza) in poems that move "just beyond the form of the haiku" (292).

Bruce Ross concludes the book with: "Burnell Lippy's Haiku in Relation to Zen" (Chapter 14). Ross describes Lippy (1944 –) as a Zen practitioner, sitting zazen two hours daily, living rustically, and creating haiku "often tinged with sabi (an aesthetic loneliness) to evoke a remoteness of consciousness, a fidelity to the things of nature" (295). Ross concludes: "If one of Zen's aims is to transcend such alienation [that separates us from the world], Lippy has effected this aim through his haiku which reveal the transparency of being if only for a moment." (304)

Kiuchi's book offers a wide range of haiku aesthetics, particularly concerning ways that poets have re-imagined the haiku. Half of the material, however, is similar to other recent collections including Yoshinobu Hakutani's *Haiku and Modernist Poetics* (2009), readable online with chapters on Noguchi, Pound, Kerouac, Wright, Sanchez, and Emanuel. Also, recent issues of *Juxta* reviewed individual books devoted to one or another of these poets.

I congratulate the editor for including a 20-page index, to help the reader navigate the richness of named poets and publications. For haiku poets that place a premium on correct words, a frustration is the book's typos, particularly names of authors, cited works, and the layout of Larry Gates' elsewhere-glorious snake-in-the-grass concrete haiku (76).

References

Hakutani, Yoshinobu. *Haiku and Modernist Poetics*. 2009. Accessed July 4 2021. <http://mbdodd.weebly.com/uploads/1/4/1/6/14162844/yoshinobu_hakutani_-_haiku_and_modernist_poetics.pdf>.

Kacian, Jim, Philip Roland, and Allan Burns, eds. *Haiku in English: The First Hundred Years*. New York: Norton, 2013.

I am grateful to Patricia J. Machmiller for commenting on a draft of this review.

Rain, Sake, and the Moon:

A Review of *The Life and Zen Haiku Poetry of Santōka Taneda*.

J. Zimmerman

> Sumita Oyama; Translated with an Introduction by William Scott Wilson. *The Life and Zen Haiku Poetry of Santōka Taneda: Japan's Most Beloved Modern Haiku Poet* (2021). Rutland, VT: Tuttle Publishing. Hardcover, 352 pages. ISBN 978-4-8053-1655-9.

The Life and Zen Haiku Poetry of Santōka Taneda, assembled by acclaimed translator and scholar William Scott Wilson, centers on his translation of Sumita Oyama's biography of the haiku poet and Zen priest Santōka Taneda[1] (1882 – 1940). The book is remarkable and rich. I recommend it to all readers interested in modern Japanese poetry and particularly to those heedful of the work and life of Santōka.

Santōka, "who lived so long at the margin of society, became a sort of beloved national resource in the years following his death" (47).

---

1. In this review I follow Wilson's format of putting the Japanese family name after given name(s). Also, in names and in haiku transliterations I write Wilson's single vowels instead of double vowels or vowels with macrons, except that *Juxta* editors have added the macron to Santōka's and Hakudō's names.

Wilson's substantial introduction describes Santōka as: "a man who could well identify with weeds: unruly, unkempt, taking sustenance from wherever he could find it, and inexorably expressing his own truth with the small irregular blossoms of what might be called 'free haiku'" (8). Indeed, Santōka's haiku often mingle his own identity with that of weeds, as in:

Yuki yuki / taoreru made no / michi no kusa ² ³

Going, going,
        right up to collapse;
    the roadside weeds (97).

I have one concern, however, that the line breaks Wilson applies to the Japanese here and throughout are unlikely to be Santōka's. They may be Wilson's own idea or perhaps they copy line breaks that Oyama chose. In contrast, this and other Santōka haiku are each laid out in a single line in a web-available Japanese transcription of Santōka notebooks, as specified in Footnote 3 and to which Japanese linguist Katsuhiko Momoi directed me (personal communications, August 2021). Hiroaki Sato adds to my caution in his introduction to his own translation of Santōka (2002): "As I keep pointing out, the majority of Japanese haiku writers regard the haiku as a one-line poem." Japanese poet and translator Emiko

---

2. Each such "transliteration" (Wilson's word) of a Santōka poem allows a reader to experience how the poem sounded to Santōka. Wilson's transliterations are not in the book but are online at the publisher's web site: www.tuttlepublishing.com/the-life-and-zen-haiku-poetry-of-Santōka-Taneda. Furthermore, that location has the poems read not only in translation but also in their original Japanese.
3. Katsuhiko Momoi (personal email, August 13, 2021) comments that this poem appears slightly differently in Volume 1 of twelve in the "Santōka's diary of begging life" online at "Aozora Bunko" or "Open Sky Collection." There, "te" is added after the second "yuki" giving "yuki yuki te." Out of copyright, the notebooks have been transcribed and proofread in Japanese by volunteers for "Aozora Bunko." Volume 1 is freely readable at: https://www.aozora.gr.jp/cards/000146/files/44913_30581.html .

Miyashita emphasizes that Santōka wrote "free verse haiku" and that when she and Paul Watsky translated their book of Santōka's haiku (2006) they created line breaks, which they inserted at kire (cutting words) that suggested grammatical breaks (personal communications, August 2021).

Wilson quotes Santōka's remark that: "Composing verse is nothing other than life" (30). He identifies and demonstrates Santōka's main influences: Seigetsu Inoue (ca. 1822–1887), Hosai Ozaki (1885–1926), Hekigodo Kawahigashi[4] (1873–1937), and Seisensui Ogiwara (1884–1976). Those free-style poets believed: "a haiku was more a matter of content than of style; what unfolded immediately before the poet became the poetry; there was no room for the 'lie' of décor or self-conscious technique" (31).

Biographer Sumita Oyama (1899–1994) was a prolific Japanese writer, a haiku poet, and "one of Santōka's greatest friends and benefactors" (9). They met in 1933 (21). Oyama's biography *Haijin Santōka no Shogai* (1984), translated as "Life of the Haiku Poet Santōka," describes the whole of "the poet's wandering and sometimes chaotic life, but also [. . .] many more of his haiku than available in Blyth's [1964] collection" (9). Oyama quotes some 325 haiku and illustrates Santōka's life story with many quotations from Santōka's journals, including this from 1930:

> A day of not walking is lonely.
> A day of not drinking is lonely.
> A day of not writing poetry is lonely (92).

Early in the biography Oyama summarizes Santōka as "a scholar, but irredeemably selfish and a sake drinker to boot" (58). Nevertheless the text shows Santōka's original yet accessible haiku and his steadfastness to writing: "To me, living is writing haiku" (280). Most readers probably ignore Santōka's less attractive personality traits.[5]

---

4. Wilson writes "Kawagihashi" (37), which is likely a typo.
5. In addition to his income from begging, the traveling Santōka received

After the biography, Wilson translates Santōka's 1940 final-year diary. The itinerant Santōka was still traveling on foot. Wilson summarizes: "Except for the island of Hokkaido in the far north, Santōka walked the length and breadth of Japan" (336) in "his nearly fifteen years of walking" (339). In a 1939 journal, Santōka recorded a seemingly typical walking day that began with a frequent presence in his haiku, rain: "it's raining [. . .] I start off after eight in the morning. I open my umbrella and start to walk. While walking, body and mind seem lighter. For me, walking is a kind of medicine" (346).

The therapy of walking appears to have encouraged Santōka not only to survive (despite his addiction to sake, his near-starvation diet, and the loss of all his teeth) but also to produce his haiku. Those often reflect his impoverishment, his need and desire to roam, and his begging in the guise of a monk for rice and enough spare change to allow him sake that evening and possibly a hot-springs bath and overnight bed. He was well known for getting drunk[6] and his desire to enjoy a "perfect" kind of drunkenness:

---

frequent and fairly regular letters and packages that included money; he let benefactors (particularly his wife, his son, and friends) know where he was going so they could send gifts to be held for him at post offices. The biography mentions several times that Santōka expressed disappointment when he did not receive a letter he expected. His main concern was for the money that was to be included. It appeared to be rare for Santōka to express solicitude for the person sending it.

6. Oyama documented that one day they were together, Santōka drank nine cups of sake while Oyama drank one (182). Sake, made by fermenting polished rice, has an alcohol content of about 18%; a traditional cup held slightly over 6 fluid ounces of sake (https://en.wikipedia.org/wiki/Sake.html). Nine cups, then, would be over 54 fluid ounces or almost half a gallon of wine.

SEVEN

Horo horo youte / ko no ha furu

Pleasantly drunk,
    falling
        leaves (70). [7]

In this translation the four words of English encapsulate the essential Santōka, a happy alcoholic, who can fall down as easily as wind-blown leaves. Wilson annotates the Japanese "*Horo horo*" as a phrase of "mimesis implying pleasantly, scatteringly, or melodiously" (73). For me, the sound also resonates with a rueful English "oh-oh" signaling imbalance or error. In addition, Santōka's Japanese shows assonance of three of its other five words with the "o" of *horo*, as well as consonance of its final word on the "r." Furthermore, the last word has ghost consonance with horo, due to the Japanese similarity of "f" and "h" in pronunciation.

Wilson reports that Santōka's poems in Japanese range widely in size, between 8 and 28 sound units (49). As noted earlier, Santōka probably wrote most of his poems in free form, unlineated, and used *kire* (rather than punctuation) to suggest grammatical breaks. However, of the poems quoted in the biography, Wilson presents only 1% of the Japanese versions in a single line; he shows roughly two-thirds in three lines and one-third in two lines. Wilson translates all the poems into a 3-line format, adds a lot of punctuation, and ends each haiku with a period. Felicitously his layout echoes on a small-scale Santōka's drunken totter: he begins each first line with capitalization, indents the second line, and staggers the third line backward.

Many of Santōka's haiku have no season word yet show haiku sensibility:

---

7. Charles Trumbull's Haiku Database (on June 17, 2021) included eight other translations of this haiku, organized in 1, 2, 3, and 5 lines. I prefer Wilson's new version due to its concision, word choice, and ragged layout.

Sukoshi / netsu ga aru kaze no naka wo / isogu

Slightly fevered,
   I hurry
     through the wind (97).

Santōka's "fever" might be a physical illness. It might also be a rapturous desire to hurry down the road to subsequent handouts and sake. While Santōka plausibly wrote this poem in a single line, Wilson presents it in the book in three vertical lines of Japanese, which he transliterates into 17 sound units (morae) in a 3-11-3 pattern. Nonetheless, this arrangement pleases my Western sensibilities because it emphasizes musicality between the first and last words, with their consonance (on "s") and their ghost consonance ("g" being the voiced version of "k").

Santōka's diary from 1940 is titled *Isso-an Nikki* ("Diary of the One-Grass Hut"). It is very engaging and brings us closest to the inner Santōka. Wilson translates it from Oyama's four-volume *Santōka no Chosakushu* ("Collection of the literary works of Santōka"). Santōka's entry for October 3, 1940, is exemplary, including not only a self-assessment with an anecdote that shows a character flaw (carelessness here), but also Santōka's last note on the essence of haiku:

> [I feel] both pleasure and embarrassment. Humiliation and shame. Gratitude, gratitude. […] I got perfectly drunk but not dead drunk. I […] did not put out the lights sufficiently for the [wartime] blackout, and was scolded by the youthful inspector.
>
> Concerning the character of haiku:
>
> * Symbolism of impression—eternality of the moment—the totality and the individual.
> * Crystallization—simplification without constriction.
> * Purification of body and mind—transparently clear.
> * Kernel, focus (331).

October 3, which was Santōka's 58th birthday though he did not mention it, was only eight days before his death in his sleep on October 11.

> *Yagate / shinuru kishiki wa / miezu yubotaru*
>
> Nothing suggests
>   they will die before long:
>   evening fireflies (109).

There are two ways in which this excellent book could have been even better. First, an index would have saved me from difficulties in finding haiku and references to specific people. Second, I would have liked the text to include the transliterations thereby giving a nonreader of Japanese the sound of the originals on first reading. Wilson does, however, make the transliterations of the biography's haiku available online (see Footnote 2) with a bonus of audio recordings "to offer non-Japanese-speaking readers a chance to recite the poems out loud, and hear how they might have sounded at the haiku parties Santōka so loved" (50).

The Japanese scholars Hiroaki Sato, Emiko Miyashita, and Katsuhiko Momoi were tremendously generous with insights on Santōka's original haiku lineation. I am grateful to Greg Longenecker and Charles Trumbull for each commenting on different early drafts of this review. I am indebted to Charles Trumbull for emailing me more than two thousand different translations (corresponding to a few hundred of Santōka's haiku) in his Haiku Database. One item I was delighted to discover from scanning those translations was a preference of Santōka (or of his translators) for the moon over sake in haiku — only 1% of the database translations mentioned sake but almost 5% mentioned the moon.

Sake wa nai / tsuki shimijimi / mite ori

No sake;
     gazing intently
at the moon (287).

References

Blyth, R.H. "Santōka." *A History of Haiku: Volume 2*. Tokyo: The Hokuseido Press, 1964. 173-188.

Santōka. *Grass and Tree Cain*. Trans. Hiroaki Sato. Illustrations Stephen Addiss. Winchester: Red Moon Press, 2002.

Santōka. *Santōka: A Translation with Photographic Images*. Trans. Emiko Miyashita and Paul Watsky. Photographs Hakudō Inoue. Tokyo: PIE Books, 2006.

Modern Matters:

A Review of *American Haiku, Eastern Philosophies, and Modernist Poetics.*

Keith Ekiss

> Yoshinobu Hakutani. *American Haiku, Eastern Philosophies, and Modernist Poetics.* Lanham, MD: Lexington Books, 2021. Hardcover. 236 pages. ISBN 978-1-7936-3450-4.

I.

Ever-attentive to suffering in nature, Kobayashi Issa once wrote:

> Do not hit the fly,
> It is praying with its hands
> And with its feet.
>   (Hakutani 111)

Picking up the theme 150 years later, Jack Kerouac responded:

> Shall I break God's commandment?
> Little fly
> Rubbing its back legs
>   (Hakutani 114)

In the years after World War II, Kerouac and fellow poets Allen Ginsberg and Gary Snyder were reading R.H. Blyth, whose monumental translations of the minimalist form did much to popularize the haiku tradition among British and American readers and writers. Ginsberg wrote in his journal: "Haiku composed in the backyard cottage at Berkeley 1955, while reading R.H. Blyth's 4 volume *Haiku*" (Hakutani 1). Snyder was studying Asian literature and dreaming of a future of Buddha-hip travelers roaming the American landscape. In *Dharma Bums*, Kerouac ventriloquizes Snyder through the character Japhy Ryder, having Ryder say:

> Think what a great world revolution will take place when East meets West finally, and it'll be guys like us that can start the thing. Think of millions of guys all over the world with rucksacks on their backs tramping around the back country and hitchhiking and bringing the word down to everybody. (Hakutani 140)

Kerouac learned from Snyder, and Ginsberg admired what Kerouac learned, writing: "Kerouac has the one sign of being a great poet, which is he's the only one in the United States who knows how to write haikus" (Hakutani 130).

The Beats valued spontaneity and improvisation, and the haiku tradition available through Blyth provided a model, albeit one based on constraint and specificity.

II.

Yoshinobu Hakutani's new book, *American Haiku, Eastern Philosophies, and Modernist Poetics*, a revision and extension of his 2009 volume *Haiku and Modernist Poetics*, and which also includes material from a 2019 book, *Jack Kerouac and the Traditions of Classic and Modern Haiku*, traces the influence of haiku on the Beats, Ezra Pound, Richard Wright, and two contemporary Black poets, Sonia Sanchez and James Emanuel. Far from a peripheral influence,

SEVEN

Hakutani sees translations of Asian literature, specifically the haiku, as central to an understanding of American poetry.

The impact of haiku through Blyth on the Beat generation represents at least a third wave of translation and influence. Starting with the Victorians in the latter half of the 19th-century, English-language translators tried to bring over the grace and precision, the attentiveness to the cycles of nature, that they found in haiku. These first generation efforts, predictably enough, read as somewhat strained and fusty by modern standards. A translation by Clara A. Walsh of a well-known poem by Bashō serves as an example: "The autumn gloaming deepens into night; / Black 'gainst the slowly-fading orange light, / On withered bough a lonely crow is sitting" (Miyamori 83). There's a long way between this effort and a more recent translation by Robert Hass: "A crow / has settled on a bare branch— / autumn evening" (Hass 13). Hakutani's chapters detailing the influence of haiku on modernism help to explain this shift in poetry and translation to a cleaner, less-adorned style.

Hakutani charts the course of one writer and translator who helped to introduce the haiku to a post-Victorian generation of poets, the modernists who centered around Ezra Pound in London in the years before World War I. Yone Noguchi, born near Nagoya in 1875, studied Victorian literature as a youth and translated 18th-century English poetry into Japanese. One of the strengths of Hakutani's book is to bring Noguchi's influence from the margin closer to the center as an influence on Ezra Pound and Imagism, the beginning of modernist poetics in English.

Noguchi's restlessness and curiosity, and his fascination with the West, lead him to San Francisco in 1893, where he fell in with the bohemian scene, living for three years near Oakland on the property of poet Joaquin Miller, reading Walt Whitman and writing Whitmanesque verse. All in all, Noguchi wrote some 90 books, many of which interpreted Japanese art and culture for a Western audience.

Noguchi returned to Japan in 1904, becoming an English professor at Keio University in Tokyo, the same college from which he'd dropped out 11 years earlier. Noguchi's travels, however, weren't over. Hakutani relates how Noguchi traveled to the U.K., lecturing at Oxford and at the Quest Society in 1914, where Pound and other Imagist poets lectured in the same year. Pound knew of Noguchi's writing, as evidenced by surviving correspondence. Responding to the gift of a book from Noguchi, Pound wrote:

> You are giving us the spirit of Japan, is it not? very much as I am trying to deliver from obscurity certain forgotten odours of Provence & Tuscany . . . . Of your country I know almost nothing — surely if the east & the west are ever to understand each other that understanding must come slowly and come first through the arts . . . . (Hakutani 48)

Hakutani reasons that among other influences, Noguchi helped Pound to understand the haiku, which in turn informed Imagism, the short-lived but influential touchstone of early 20th-century poetry.

Pound himself acknowledged his debt to Japanese verse in an essay he wrote two years after the publication of one of his most widely anthologized poems.

> In a Station of the Metro
>
> The apparition of these faces in the crowd;
> Petals on a wet, black bough.

Pound refers to this poem as "a hokku-like sentence." Seizing on Pound's use of the word "hokku," as opposed to *haiku*, Hakutani concludes that Pound most likely came to that term through Noguchi's influence, since this was Noguchi's preferred term. Pound's fellow Imagists, T.E. Hulme and F.S. Flint, employed the terms *haiku* and *haikai*, which they in turn received through French translations of Japanese poetry.

In the same essay on the origins of "In a Station of the Metro," Pound translates a hokku by the 15th-century Japanese poet Arakida Moritake: "The fallen blossom falls back to its branch: / a butterfly" that Noguchi had previously translated and published before Pound's essay. "I thought I saw the fallen leaves / Returning to their branches: / Alas, butterflies were they" (Hakutani 68). Pound's habit of clarifying what he liked in poetry from other languages is firmly on display in this re-translation. Clearly the haiku, still relatively new to English language readers, wrapped itself around the DNA of modern poetry. We are all to varying extents modernists and the haiku, in its journey from east to west, is woven into that legacy.

III.

In addition to his writings on the history of haiku in English, Hakutani is also the editor of *This Other World*, the landmark edition of Richard Wright's haiku. Hakutani draws on this knowledge for two chapters on the novelist's poetry, along with material on the haiku's history that appears both in the Wright book and in the present volume.

Wright and his wife moved to France in 1947 to escape, as one writer noted, "the humiliation they faced as an interracial couple in New York City." Except for brief visits in 1949 and 1950, Wright never returned to the United States. In the years before his death in 1960, Wright was often fatigued and ill in bed. One day, he picked up a poetry book given to him by a South African Beatnik, Sinclair Beiles. The book was a copy of Blyth. Over the last 18 months of his life, Wright composed some 4,000 (strictly syllabic) haiku, of which 817 are collected in Hakutani's *This Other World*.

Hakutani connects Wright's deep engagement with haiku to a larger search for Black identities across the diaspora. Reading J.B. Danquah's *The Akan Doctrine of God*, "Wright was persuaded of the African belief that spirits reside in inanimate objects like trees, stones, and rivers" (Hakutani 98). This belief, Hakutani continues, maps to Shintoist conceptions of animism that form part of the long cultural history of haiku.

Wright's poetry, which Hakutani sees as absorbing traditional notions of *wabi* (physical poverty, in Hakutani's telling) and *sabi* (loneliness and quietude), give way as the tradition continues to the blues haiku of Sonia Sanchez and the jazz haiku of James Emanuel.

Sanchez makes a space in her poetry for Black speech, blending the compressed forms announced in the title of this poem.

> Blues Haiku
>
> let me be yo wil
> derness let me be you wind
> blowing you all day.
> (Hakutani 164)

The form also carries forward for Sanchez the traditions of Black poetry, as in the following poem with its deliberate echoes, Hakutani informs us, of Langston Hughes's "The Negro Speaks of Rivers."

> mixed with day and sun
> i crouched in the earth carry
> you like a dark river.
> (Hakutani 169)

The blues become jazz in the haiku of James Emanuel, poems which both reference the history of jazz and incorporate the spontaneity the Beats were searching for so many years ago.

SEVEN

> Dizzy's bellows pumps.
> Jazz balloon inflates, floats high.
> Earth listens, stands by.
> (Hakutani 188)

And:

> EVERYTHING is jazz:
> snails, jails, rails, tales, males, females,
> snow-white cotton bales.
> (Hakutani 188-189)

Hakutani picks up on the similarities between collective improvisation and linked verse, noting that, "In light of the relation of self and community, jazz also bears a strong resemblance to *renga*, fifteenth-century Japanese linked verse, from which haiku evolved" (Hakutani 185).

The Irish poet Eavan Boland, who taught for many years in the United States before her death in 2020, once said that the movement in American poetry is from the margin to the center. The best contributions of *American Haiku, Eastern Philosophies, and Modernist Poetics* lie in Hakutani's edging stories from that margin closer toward the center. Noguchi's influence on Pound is a compelling story, and helps to widen our understanding of the multivalent cultural influences occurring on the eve of World War I. His spotlight on the presence of haiku in poetic practice among African-American poets expands and complicates our notions of Black poetic traditions. Although you'll find much of Hakutani's material available in other works, and there are better introductions to haiku in Steven D. Carter's *Haiku Before Haiku* and Haruo Shirane's *Traces of Dreams*, Hakutani has opened the door for further studies of the haiku and Beat, modernist, and Black poetics.

Works Cited

Hakutani, Yoshinobu. *American Haiku, Eastern Philosophies, and Modernist Poetics*. Lanham, MD: Lexington Books, 2021.

Hass, Robert. *The Essential Haiku: Versions of Bashō, Buson, and Issa*. Hopewell, NJ: The Ecco Press, 1994.

Miyamori, Asatarō. *Classic Haiku: An Anthology of Poems by Bashō and His Followers*. Mineola, NY: Dover Publications, Inc., 2002.

Poet/Artist: Amiri Baraka

Juxta *Contributors*

Amiri BARAKA, also known as LeRoi Jones, was an American author of provocative works that assiduously presented the experiences of Black Americans in a white-dominated society. He is often referred to as the "Godfather" of the Black Arts Movement. His books include *Preface to a Twenty Volume Suicide Note* (1961) and *The Autobiography of LeRoi Jones/Amiri Baraka* (1984). He taught at Columbia, Yale, and SUNY Stony Brook, where he was emeritus professor of Africana studies.

Keith EKISS is a Jones Lecturer in Creative Writing at Stanford University. He is the author of *Pima Road Notebook* and translator of two works by the Costa Rican poet Eunice Odio, *Territory of Dawn: The Selected Poems of Eunice Odio* and *The Fire's Journey*. He is the past recipient of fellowships and residencies from the Bread Loaf Writers' Conference, Community of Writers' Conference, Millay Colony for the Arts, Santa Fe Art Institute, and the Petrified Forest National Park.

Josh HOCKENSMITH is a writer, book artist, and librarian who has worked with haiku since the 1990s when a student at the University of Richmond. He helped found the Richmond Haiku Workshop, which published *South by Southeast* 1999–2013. He is interested in book arts, the history and future of the book, and literary translation. He is the library assistant at Sloane Art Library at the University of North Carolina-Chapel Hill, where he is also working toward an MA in Art History.

Adam L. KERN had things other than haiku on his mind as a high-school exchange student in Japan. He became less oblivious while studying Japanese literature at the University of Minnesota, the University of Kyoto, and Harvard University (where he earned a Ph.D. before joining the faculty). His publications include *The Penguin Book of Haiku* and *Manga from the Floating World*. He is Professor of Japanese Literature and Visual Culture at the University of Wisconsin-Madison.

Amanda MONTELEONE is a Ph.D. candidate in the Department of English at the University of Texas at Arlington, where she currently teaches. Her interest in English-language haiku began with her study of Gerald Vizenor's writings in a graduate course on Native American literature. She has presented papers on ethnomusicologist Frances Densmore and early Cherokee writer John Rollin Ridge. Her current research focuses on modernities in East Asian literature and popular culture.

Ce ROSENOW is the co-author with Maurice Hamington of *Care Ethics and Poetry* and the co-editor with Bob Arnold of *The Next One Thousand Years: The Selected Poems of Cid Corman*. Her essays have appeared in various collections and journals including recent publications in *American Haiku: New Readings*, *African American Haiku: Cultural Visions*, and *The Journal of Ethnic American Literature*. She is the former president of the Haiku Society of America.

Crystal Simone SMITH is the author of two poetry chapbooks, *Routes Home* (Finishing Line Press, 2013) and *Running Music* (Longleaf Press, 2014) and is widely published in poetry journals. She is an alumna of the Callaloo Creative Writing Workshop and the Yale Summer Writers Conference. She holds an MFA from Queens University of Charlotte and lives in Durham, NC where she teaches English Composition and Creative Writing. She is the Managing Editor of Backbone Press.

John (Jianqiang) ZHENG is the author of *A Way of Looking*, *Enforced Rustication in the Chinese Cultural Revolution*, and *Delta Sun*. He is also the editor of *Conversations with Dana Gioia*, *African American Haiku: Cultural Visions*, *Sonia Sanchez's Poetic Spirit through Haiku*, and *The Other World of Richard Wright*.

J. ZIMMERMAN was featured in *A New Resonance* 8 (2013), the same year she invented the "Buson 100" haiku challenge. She was the first Poet in Residence for the Cabrillo Festival of Contemporary Music. Her article "Gender of Poets Winning Haiku and Senryu Contests" appeared in *Presence* (2019); its companion article "Gender of Haiku Poets Published in Journals: Game-On, Ladies?" appeared in *Modern Haiku* (2020). Her post-doc research was on the moon rocks at Washington University.

Juxta *Staff*

The haiku and haiga of Stephen ADDISS have appeared in galleries around the world. Lately he has been concentrating on ink-cuts (a form of paintilligraphy) and wood-fired teabowls. His books include *Cloud Calligraphy, A Haiku Menagerie, The Art of Zen, Haiga: Haiku-Painting, The Art of Chinese Calligraphy, Haiku People, A Haiku Garden, Haiku Humor, Tao Te Ching, Japanese Calligraphy, Haiku: An Anthology*, and *The Art of Haiku*.

DAVID GRAYSON has been writing haiku and senryu for twenty years. He authored *Discovering Fire: Haiku & Essays* (Red Moon Press, 2016), and edited *Full of Moonlight* (HSA 2016 Members' Anthology). He has been featured in *A New Resonance 6* (Red Moon Press, 2009), *My Neighbor* (Two Autumns Press, 2009) and *Spring Haiku in the Park 2018* (Yuki Teikei Society). He edited two volumes in the Two Autumns book series. He lives in the San Francisco Bay Area with his family.

JOSH HOCKENSMITH is a writer, book artist, and librarian who has worked with haiku since the 1990s when a student at the University of Richmond. He helped found the Richmond Haiku Workshop, which publllished *South by Southeast* 1999–2013. He is interested in book arts, the history and future of the book, and literary translation. He is the library assistant at Sloane Art Library at the University of North Carolina-Chapel Hill, where he is also working toward an MA in Art History.

JIM KACIAN is founder and president of The Haiku Foundation (2009), founder and owner of Red Moon Press (1993), editor-in-chief of *Haiku in English: The First Hundred Years* (W. W. Norton, 2013), and managing editor of *Juxtapositions* since its inception in 2015. His latest book of haiku and sequences is *after / image* (Red Moon Press, 2018), and his latest collaboration is with Terry Ann Carter (paper arts) and Claudia Brefeld (commentary), *the endangered C* (Red Moon Press, 2021).

Adam L. KERN had things other than haiku on his mind as a high-school exchange student in Japan. He became less oblivious while studying Japanese literature at the University of Minnesota, the University of Kyoto, and Harvard University (where he earned a Ph.D. before joining the faculty). His publications include *The Penguin Book of Haiku* and *Manga from the Floating World*. He is Professor of Japanese Literature and Visual Culture at the University of Wisconsin-Madison.

CE ROSENOW is the co-author with Maurice Hamington of *Care Ethics and Poetry* and the co-editor with Bob Arnold of *The Next One Thousand Years: The Selected Poems of Cid Corman*. Her essays have appeared in various collections and journals including recent publications in *American Haiku: New Readings*, *African American Haiku: Cultural Visions*, and *The Journal of Ethnic American Literature*. She is the former president of the Haiku Society of America.

DAVE RUSSO's haiku have appeared in *Frogpond*, *Modern Haiku*, *Acorn*, and other journals. He is included in the *New Resonance 5* anthology from Red Moon Press. He organizes events for the North Carolina Haiku Society and is the web administrator for NCHS and The Haiku Foundation, and is a founding member of both.

CRYSTAL SIMONE SMITH is the author of four poetry chapbooks including *Wildflowers: Haiku, Senryu, and Haibun* (2016). She is also a co-author of *One Windows Light: A Collection of Haiku*, Unicorn Press, (2018). Her work has appeared in numerous journals including: *Callaloo*, *Nimrod*, *Modern Haiku*, *Frogpond*, *The Heron's Nest*, and *Acorn*. She is the Founder and Managing Editor of Backbone Press.

Made in the USA
Middletown, DE
01 November 2021